RIDE TO
THE SKIES

RIDE TO THE SKIES

GEORGE PAYIKAD

PARTRIDGE
A Penguin Company

Partridge books may be ordered through booksellers or by contacting:

Partridge India
Penguin Books India Pvt.Ltd
11, Community Centre, Panchsheel Park, New Delhi 110017
India
www.partridgepublishing.com
Phone: 000.800.10062.62

CONTENTS

HOW IT ALL STARTED

It all started a long time back. The wish and urge to ride in the unforgiving and wild mountains of India. For as long as I can remember I have been a motorcycle person. I believe that true freedom can be felt only when riding a motorcycle. I also believe that cars are useful only under three circumstances; firstly, if you are out shopping—it is much more easier to bring groceries home in a car; secondly, if it is raining—nothing is more annoying than going to work or anywhere else for that matter, all soaking wet and not to mention the difficulty in seeing the road, unmindful people in cars, getting delayed for meetings and appointments, etc. and lastly, if you have children—It is just not safe to ride a motorcycle with more than two people, irrespective of how small the third person is. Now the last problem, I have not yet had to deal with, the first and second problems are never permanent, so I still prefer a motorcycle. The month is January, the year twenty thirteen. I was sitting behind a computer for more than 8 hours a day and 5 days a week. Life was becoming too predictable; it was as though my life was on auto-pilot and I had no way of switching it off. Something had to be done; I knew it would not be difficult to find that elusive spark of adventure I was looking for; it was not like I had to re-invent the wheel.

My name is George. I am working with a company in Hyderabad, India, which is at the top of its field. I was happy and loved by all (At least I hope so—and would like to think so). I worked with a small core team of people with similar mind sets and a great attitude. Some, however, are different. I was one of them, the few that had a wild streak and the urge for adventure. My mother always told me that I was not made for a quiet life. I was always doing something or the other; 90% of the time getting myself into trouble.

Along with me three others—friends and colleagues; Anoop, Srikant and Akash, decided we needed to do something, which was out of the ordinary. It would cost us money and take time for us to do something worthwhile, something noticeable enough to bring a change to my monotonous existence! After lots of thinking and deliberation we decided we would go on a road trip. Hit the open road with the wind running through our hair and without a care in the world. Almost everybody who owns a good motorcycle wants to ride in the mountains. Some of the highest mountains in the world are located in northern India and they are a part of the Himalayan Mountain Range. Being the world's highest mountain chain, the Himalayas is best known worldwide for its great height, complex geologic structure, snow-capped peaks, glaciers, deep river gorges, and rich vegetation. 'Himalaya' means 'Home of Snow', and it is obvious why, the snow never melts on their high peaks. Nine of the ten highest peaks in the world are a part of this mountain range including three of the world's highest mountains, Mount Everest (8848 meters), which is on the Nepal-Tibet border; followed by, K2 or Mount Godwin Austen (8,611 meters), located on the border between China and Jammu and Kashmir, and the third highest peak, Kanchenjunga (8,598 meters) on the Nepal-India border. The Himalayan mountain range is by far the most sought after by adventurists in India and equally so by avid bikers, the most challenging mountain roads in India are in these mountains; and the best amongst them are the roads that lead up to Leh in Ladhak, a beautiful place in Jammu and Kashmir—A place that looks like it was pulled right out of a calendar. I cannot think of a more apt description. Leh is a place that is frequented by lots of vacationers, some who want to get away from the searing heat in the lower states, where temperatures can go up to 45 degrees in the peak of summer or like most others, on a holiday with their families and friends. Of all the kinds of people who visit, Leh is best known for the hordes of bikers who ride up every year in the summer after the snow melts and the roads open up. They all ride for various reasons, some to beat the heat, some for the challenge and others purely for the thrill of the ride, the freedom, the fear and the uncertainty that waits around every corner. Leh was chosen as our destination.

Planning began in early 2013. It was going to be three motorcycles and four people. There was Akash, who owned a Royal Enfield Classic 500 'Desert Storm', Anoop and his Royal Enfield

'Electra', me with my Thunderbird and then there was Srikant, who did not have his motorcycle as yet because of the crazy amount of time that had to be spent waiting for the motorcycle to be delivered. As far as we knew, there was no other motorcycle we trusted to take us up till Leh and bring us back without giving too many problems. Leh was a good two thousand seven hundred kilometres (about 1650 miles) from Hyderabad by road; and that is just up to Leh. Reasonable riding would mean that it would take six days to ride up to Leh; the roads being non-existent in most places. Cheap accommodation can be found all along the way and our calculations showed we would need approximately forty five thousand rupees per head to make it to Leh and back. We were then presented with our next problem, six days up and six days down would total up to twelve days on the road and we wanted at least two days at Leh, which totalled up to fourteen days, that would mean we would need to take at least two weeks off from work. Some of us did not have sufficient leave to our credit and others could not be away from work that long because of various client commitments. We had reached our first impasse. We needed to re think our plan before we even actually started to plan! The only thing we knew for sure was that we would be riding our own motorcycles rather than get to Leh and rent motorcycles that we are not familiar with! We knew our motorcycles inside out and knew it was the safer option.

Flashback—2012, June—I booked my very own Royal Enfield, a Thunderbird 350 and then began the wait; demand was way too high for the supply to keep up. In January 2013, seven months after I first decided to make one my own, I got the call from the dealership . . . My motorcycle was ready for delivery. I am now a proud owner of a beautiful black Royal Enfield Thunderbird. The Chennai based company was trying hard to keep up with the ever increasing demand. Royal Enfield is a legend in itself and the brand is a cult in India with a legacy that spans for over half a century. Way back in 1955, the Indian government looked for a suitable motorcycle for its police and army. I honestly do not know what kind of competition was available back in the 1950's, but the Bullet was the motorcycle that was picked. The Indian government placed a colossal order of 800—350cc Bullets, an understandably enormous order for the time. In the same year, the 'Redditch Company' partnered with 'Madras Motors' in India, forming 'Enfield India' to assemble the motorcycles under licence in Chennai. In 1957 tooling equipment was sold to Enfield India so that they could manufacture components and start full scale production and not just assembly. Production ceased in 1970 and the company was dissolved in 1971. Remaining tooling and equipment of the Redditch Company was auctioned off. Meanwhile the Bullet 350 continued to be manufactured in India. In 1990, Enfield India entered into a strategic alliance with the Eicher Group, and later merged with it in 1994. It was during this merger that the name Enfield India changed to Royal Enfield. Royal Enfield India is still manufacturing in India and is being sold in India and is also being exported to Europe as well as America and Australia and is now the oldest motorcycle brand in the world still in production with the Bullet model enjoying the longest motorcycle production run of all time. Anybody who strived to ride and be free with wind blowing through their hair owned or wanted to own a Royal Enfield. Then came the influx of foreign manufactures, they were selling motorcycles with bigger engine capacities and better ergonomics. The legend slowly began to fade away or so it seemed. But the fact that a person who wanted a Royal Enfield bought a Royal Enfield was its saving grace. Over time the technology was upgraded; parts and the machine itself became more reliable than ever. The thump and feeling of freedom that runs down your spine and into your boots was never going to die as long as loyal riders were kept happy. Most enthusiasts learnt the love and passion for these motorcycles from their fathers and brothers, there was barely a family where someone did not own an Enfield. But, society had changed since my father last rode his vehicle, motorcycles that were restricted to men and boys began to appeal to women and in the blink of an eye the gap was bridged! Women started to own and ride motorcycles. Suddenly everybody wanted to own a motorcycle, men, women and teenagers all wanted motorcycles, but again only a few dared to get an Enfield, some too scared and the others just could not afford the hefty price tag that came along with these beauties. Owning an Enfield is almost a luxury in an economy that almost entirely survives on public transport and only looks towards motorcycles that are ridiculously fuel efficient! Within a month of getting my motorcycle, I had gone on my first road trip. We rode from Hyderabad in Andhra Pradesh to Bidar in Karnataka, a mere 150 kilometres, we had to keep in mind that the motorcycles were new and could not be ridden for too long and we had to keep the speed below 60kmph. It was a one day trip. The motorcycles handled like a charm. Now, more than a year after we rode to

Bidar, my motorcycle is over a year old and well broken in. I had not experienced any mechanical problems other than an occasional loose nut every now and then. We could ride for long distances at sustained speeds.

We were looking for alternative plans ever since we realized the fourteen day plan would not work. Then we came up with a new plan that would require us to take just six days off from work, less than half compared to the original plan. We would transport our motorcycles up to Delhi by truck, fly to Delhi and then ride the remaining 1100 Kilometres from Delhi to Leh. It sounded like the most practical of all the other options we thought of. After shipping costs, we would still be saving money, considering the current rate of petrol and on lodging. Twice in between the time we started making plans and the day we actually got our motorcycles ready to ship, I almost pulled out of the ride for some insignificant reason or the other. Now that it is all over and done I am extremely glad that I did finally go on the trip.

On the 14th of May we left our motorcycles in the care of Mr Deepak Singh of Sri. Vinesh Logistics. He said it would take anywhere from 10-14 days for the motorcycles to reach Gurgaon. Our flight tickets to Delhi were also booked. That was the first time all of us realized that this was happening! Our long awaited and meticulously planned ride was going live in two weeks. Life went on as usual; every now and then we would shop for a little something we thought we needed, ranging from thermal wear to rope to super glue. My plan to write this book also came into my head at around this time; I decided it would be a memoir of sorts. There are gaps in my knowledge of the whole trip, but I have pictures to help me remember things and also the internet, in case I cannot remember if a town, village or mountain came in the order I think it did. What you are reading now is my very own account of how our whole journey went and to make it a little interesting, I have also gleaned some facts about a few places we stayed at, from friends, sign boards along the way (of which I took pictures), other tourists and of course the internet as well.

DAY 1

MAY 23, 2013

T he long awaited day had finally arrived; I could not contain my excitement. There was just the eight hours of work separating us from our road trip. It took forever, but finally the day ended and we were on our way to the airport. Our Air India flight AI 127 took off at 8:55PM from Hyderabad's Shamshabad International Airport, the night was clear and we were headed straight for the capital city of New Delhi. Two hours and 15 minutes later we landed at New Delhi's terminal 3. It was a sultry 40 degrees and it was past 11 PM. We literally ran to baggage claim to get our bags and be on our way. The cargo company had promised to give us our motorcycles as soon as we reached, even if it was going to be late. Our bags were amongst the first off the plane and on to the belt—all except one, we had to wait for a good twenty minutes before it finally rolled out onto the belt in front of us. We grabbed it and made a bee line for the pre-paid taxi counter. We were warned beforehand that cabbies in Delhi may swindle people who were not familiar with the city. From the airport at New Delhi, we headed to Gurgaon, the largest city in Haryana and also its industrial and financial center. The cargo company thankfully kept their promise and remained open, because by the time we finally found the place it was well past midnight, after we got two motorcycles unloaded from the large containers they had been sitting and dusted them as best as we could in the darkness. We started them, Anoop's motorcycle started up in a couple of kicks, I had a little trouble with mine, I found the cause of the problem after a few minutes of kicking— there was no petrol in it. It was bone dry. Cargo companies drain the fuel tank of all petrol to prevent any accidents; it is also a legal requirement. Why only my motorcycle's tank was drained I do not know. The one running motorcycle was sent to buy some petrol while Akash and I waited with my motorcycle and the luggage. After a good twenty minutes the rescue party came back with petrol. We finally got both motorcycles started and headed towards the second cargo company that had transported a third motorcycle from Bangalore in Karnataka, unfortunately for us, the company said they would not give the motorcycle and switched off their phones. Akash would have to wait till morning before he would get his motorcycle. Having nothing else to do, we decided to call it a day. We found a hotel nearby, had a shower, chatted for a little while and went to bed. Day 1 ended without being able to accomplish our goal of getting all three motorcycles. All we did was end up riding about thirty kilometres within Gurgaon itself.

DAY 2

MAY 24, 2013

Before we went to bed the previous night, we decided we would first pick up the third motorcycle, meet a few friends who are working in Delhi and finally pick up a few last minute supplies before we left Delhi and headed for the union territory of Chandigarh.

Chandigarh is the only city that acts as a capital to two different states—Haryana and Punjab. (While I am writing this, the Indian government has decided to split the state of Andhra Pradesh into two different states and if this comes through successfully, then by the time this book comes into the hands of my readers, Hyderabad will probably be the second city that is capital to two different states—Telangana and Andhra). Now back to our trip, we started from Gurgaon at eight in the morning, picked up the third motorcycle and headed towards Mayur Vihar; it was literally on the other side of the city. We finally reached and by then the sun was up and mercilessly beating down on us, it was hot and miserable and to add to all the misery was the traffic, dust and incessant honking of other impatient motorists. We finally made it to Mayur Vihar (Thank God for GPS), finished our business there and went to meet the other friend. On a normal day, considering the distance we had yet to travel and the heat, we would have skipped meeting him, but apparently in Jammu & Kashmir, for security reasons pre-paid cell phones do not work and we just had two post-paid phones amongst the four of us. The meeting with the friend was to get a third SIM for us to use. Once we met him and collected the SIM, we started towards our last destination before leaving Delhi—Jhilmil Colony; this was the place where we planned on picking up our remaining supplies—a carrier, jerry cans for fuel, a better first aid kit and a puncture kit, a single stop where we could procure all these things under one roof. On the way we stopped to get something to drink and while we were waiting one of us decided it would be a smart thing to call the place and then go, so a call was made and as it turned out, the carrier and jerry can was not available because we forgot to confirm our requirement and the next availability was in 3 days. In one way it was good, since we did not have to find the place and we could leave the city right away. However, not going to the shop is something we regretted two days later—why I will tell you as we progress. We finally started for Chandigarh, stopping on the way to buy a helmet as the cargo company lost one of ours. It was well past noon and blisteringly hot, the sun was continuously beating down on us from above and the heat radiating from the asphalt below was getting too much, without too much argument we decided to take a break, we pulled over beside the road and got ourselves some cold water—we finished five litres in all and were still thirsty and hot. We rested by the roadside for a while and continued—the ride was uneventful and hot till we realized one of us was missing from the small group, we pulled over and waited for the missing rider to catch up, but nothing happened, luckily we were still within city limits and our phones were still working, we called him, he was hopelessly lost and in completely the opposite direction from where we were, we tried to get him to ask for directions and come to where we were, but it was hopeless. We then decided to set out and find him instead, it was imperative that we stayed together, the city was alien and all of us except one were not that good in Hindi. We finally found him beside the Nizamuddin railway station. The road that led to the station was jam-packed with traffic and it was a pain trying to negotiate through the traffic and multitudes of people and cattle. We finally were able to regroup. We used the opportunity to grab some food and then set off. By the time we left Delhi city limits and were headed towards Chandigarh, it was well past three and still ridiculously hot. Once we hit the open highway, it got so hot, that we had to stop, as our hands were literally getting scorched in the heat. When we started I had decided against wearing a jacket assuming that it would only get hotter. That was a very bad assumption. The place we stopped was a small dhaba by the highway. Dhabas are small roadside hotels that serve the local cuisine and are more frequently known to serve as truck stops. We finished a few bottles of cold water as soon as we stopped and then I fell asleep.

I woke up an hour and a half later, it was relatively cooler and the sun was not as hot. Anoop, Srikant and Akash had lunch while I was asleep. I too ate a few mouthfuls after I woke up and we set out straight for Chandigarh. It was a nice comfortable ride and we began to make up time averaging 80kmph. We crossed over into Punjab a little after the sun went down and sometime after that we were soon in Chandigarh.

To be honest it is one of the most well planned cities I have ever had the privilege of being in, unfortunately we would not have sufficient time to explore the city and I later found out from a friend and old colleague we met there that it is the first planned city in India, and is known internationally for its architecture and urban design. A quick search online proved him correct. The city has projects designed by architects such as Le Corbusier, Pierre Jeanneret, Jane Drew, and Maxwell Fry. It has amongst the highest per capita income for any state or union territory in India and is also reported to be the cleanest city as of 2010. Our friend who is from Jalandhar, an hour away from Chandigarh met us and took us to a hotel where we called it a day. Just to give you an idea of how hot it was, the four of us drank about 30 litres of water between us and did not have a need to relieve ourselves even once, all the way from Delhi till we were in our hotel in Chandigarh. We were dirty, extremely tired and could think of nothing other than having a cold shower, turning on the AC and hitting the bed. Thus ended day two, we had covered two hundred and fifty kilometres in a little less than eight hours. One of the plans we had was to try and make it to Manali on day 2 itself. Maybe it was good that we left Delhi late and that the temperature was high, because if everything had worked according to plan we probably would have pushed ourselves to reach Manali and then end up getting worn out in the middle of the mountains with no place to stay.

DAY 3

MAY 25, 2013

We awoke early, our destination was Manali in Himachal Pradesh, before that we had one more thing to do. Since Chandigarh is a union territory petrol is cheaper when compared to other states in India. If we tanked up the motorcycles before leaving Chandigarh, we would save around seven rupees per litre an overall savings of about hundred rupees. Our friend escorted us out of town and till the turn off, from where we would head to Manali and he would continue home to Jalandhar. Once we said our good byes and parted ways we stopped for breakfast, we had delicious aloo parathas and nice hot tea. An 'Aloo Paratha' is basically unleavened dough stuffed with a mixture of mashed potato and other spices, which is rolled out and cooked on a hot tawa with butter or ghee and served with yoghurt. The weather was pleasant and we were looking forward to the day's ride. Within an hour of breakfast we began to climb up and towards the Kullu bypass road, it was a two lane, winding mountain road that was mostly used by slow moving heavy vehicle traffic. A little later the worst fear of anyone travelling long distances materialized, we come up on a huge traffic jam; one side of the road is the mountain and the other side a sheer drop. There were at least a hundred cars and trucks backed up. This is where the benefit of a two wheeler plays best, we began to weave through the backed up traffic to get ahead of the line of cars, on a normal day we would not do it and neither do any of us endorse such behaviour, but we needed to cover a long distance and since traffic was completely stopped we slowly snaked our way between all the cars and trucks, till we came upon the reason for the whole line of backed up vehicles. A truck and trailer was teetering on the edge of the road, another 10 feet and that would be it for the truck, fortunately or unfortunately for everyone involved the only thing it did was block one whole lane of traffic, we got past it and continued on with the whole lane to ourselves since all other vehicles were stuck behind us. A little later we came upon another traffic jam, again the offender was a truck that blocked the road, and this time weaving through traffic was not as easy because every other vehicle on the road wanted to get out of the traffic. We had to cut across between lanes of traffic and then I came up on a motorcycle lying on its side and one of the guys standing beside it, making it the first spill for the ride. Thankfully Akash who was riding the motorcycle was unhurt, other motorists helped us pick up the motorcycle and we were on our way again. A short while later we passed the turn off towards Shimla. We continued on our way, stopping occasionally for a break, to rest, take in the scenery and finally for lunch. We had a nice hearty meal and started again. The roads got better other than for a few potholes around which we negotiated with ease. As the ride progressed we began to ride beside the 'Beas' river. It was still a little hot, but tolerable and as we kept heading further up the road the weather kept getting cooler. We were riding along on a mountain road and suddenly we came upon a tunnel, it was three kilometres long, and very cold inside it. On the other side it was like a whole different place. The weather was no longer hot and it was also drizzling. We stopped for a few moments to see if the rain was getting worse. Thankfully for us, it stopped drizzling. We continued the push on towards Manali, passing numerous droves of goats and sheep that slowed down traffic. After about an hour, we finally crossed over into Manali after paying the green tax of hundred rupees per motorcycle. Manali is a beautiful, small and crowded place, the roads too small and narrow for the hordes of tourists that throng the place. There is no way I can actually describe Manali, without doing injustice to it. Anything I say will fall short of the beauty it holds in itself. There are parks, orchards, gardens, rivers and so many other things, the list is endless. We kept riding around town, looking for a hotel as close as we could on the road that led out of town. After a few minutes, we found a hotel called 'River Inn' which was on the banks of the Beas. The room was big enough for all of us to fit comfortably, with room for more. It was clean and well within our budget. From our room we could see and hear the 'Beas' thundering its way down the mountain. On the other side of the river is the road that leads straight up into town and it was packed with cars slowly making their way through the traffic. I do not think the designers of the town ever imagined that there would be so many cars and the roads would become as incapable of handling the traffic. After we all had a nice hot shower, I went out to find a petrol station. Once I was back, Anoop and Akash left to get fuel for their motorcycles and along with that buy dinner. We had chicken biryani or at least that is what we think it was. It was very different from the biryani that is available in the south and was almost like gruel with chicken and a bunch of spices. We ate as much as we dared to eat knowing very well that we would require every bit of energy we could muster for the days ahead. We had to be up at least by 2 am the next morning to be able to cover the 52 kilometres to the dreaded Rohtang pass and cross it by 6am after which traffic movement would be restricted. Day three ended with us covering 300 kilometres in about eleven hours.

DAY 4

MAY 26, 2013

The alarm woke us up at 2am; it was one of the hardest things I personally had to do since we had started riding. The weather was perfect for sleeping and I was dog tired from the previous days ride. We pulled ourselves very reluctantly out from under the warm blankets and set about getting ready. We finished our ablutions, put on our warm clothes and picked up all the bags and started on our way down to where the motorcycles were parked. To our dismay we found the exit door locked and nobody around to let us out. We tried using the telephone in our room to call down to the reception but nobody answered. We had no time to waste, so I went in search of someone to open the doors and let us out and finally found someone fast asleep in the kitchen. I woke him up asked him to open the door, after which we carried our bags down to the motorcycles. When I was rolling my motorcycle out from where it was parked I realized the front tyre was flat thought not fully, so we figured it was not a puncture and that somebody had let out the air, we suspected a group of young men we had an argument with over parking the previous night. It was dark and there was nobody around, so we decided to see what could be done. The pump we had proved handy and we were able to fill air into the tyre, we waited for a couple of minutes to see if the air would escape, noting happened. We cursed the men we thought had let out the air and started. It was quarter to three. Our immediate goal was to pass Rohtang pass by 6 am. The bell boy at the hotel told us it would take anywhere from two hours to three hours to cross the pass and considering we had to cross before six, we had left so early. Rohtang literally means 'Pile of Corpses', because of the sheer number of people who died due to the cold while trying to cross the pass. It is a natural divide between the sub-humid/humid Kullu Valley with a primarily Hindu culture (in the south), and the arid/semi-arid high-altitude Lahaul and Spiti valleys with a Buddhist culture in the north. It is only open from late May to November, rest of the time it is covered in snow, making it un-motorable and dangerous. The unpredictable weather conditions that prevail on the pass can have a person stranded in a blizzard without any warning and sometimes for days on end. There is a current project being undertaken by the Indian government to build a tunnel under the pass, which on completion will reduce the travel time from the current 6-7 hours to about half an hour. It will be a great boost for the economy of the north, but the primary use will be to keep the army camps supplied throughout the year. Once the tunnel is completed and thrown open to traffic, the challenge that we and other motorists like us enjoy will be a thing of the past. Thank God, we are doing it now, before it is too late. When we started, we were the only motorcycles on the road and it was pitch dark and as quiet as death! I was leading, since my motorcycle was the only one with upgraded 'High Intensity Discharge' (HID) Xenon headlamps, it lit up the place like the sun. On normal highways 52 kilometres would ideally be less than an hour at moderate speeds, but as soon as we started we hit the mountain and the climb started. There were no other motorists on the road and the only activity we passed were shepherds herding their scores of sheep to God knows where! Being on two wheelers the ride up the mountain was fast and immense fun—as we gained altitude it started to get colder and we came across the first truck struggling to pull its fully laden weight up the mountain, the road was in exceptionally good condition and we were making good time. After a while the asphalt gave away to good old mud and dirt, this was also not too bad as we were amongst the first few vehicles to use it, the road was still frozen hard, in sections however the weight of trucks that had passed minutes ahead of us had broken up the road and made it a mucky mess. By half past five we had crested the mountain, considering all the hue and cry that was being made in Manali, we expected to see a check post or at least a guard to check our papers, but it was isolated and the rows of white army barracks looked like a ghost town, not a living thing stirred in the biting cold, there was just the constant thump of our motorcycles to keep us company. By now there was enough light and I dropped to the middle of the pack, with Anoop and Srikant leading up front. As I rounded a bend, I saw the back of their motorcycle begin to slide out from under them and immediately slowed to a crawl, Anoop's years of experience riding such roads kicked in and he saved it just in time. A few more seconds and the two of them would have been on the ground. We came to a complete stop and turned around just in time to see Akash and his motorcycle come crashing around the bend, the road was wet and icy and our inexperience riding in such conditions showed through. It will make a point to say now, that Akash's motorcycle was almost brand new and had a little over 700 kilometres on the odometer when we started from Delhi. The bags strapped to the motorcycle prevented it from hitting the road surface and getting damaged; it also prevented the weight of the motorcycle from coming down on his leg. Akash jumped up and away from the motorcycle. Srikant and I ran over to pick up his motorcycle as precious petrol was leaking out from the top of the tank. A quick check of Akash turned up only a slightly damaged ego, the crash guard of the motorcycle took a little damage, but since that is what it is meant for we said nothing more and continued, more so to get out of the cold and from the middle of the single lane road. As we continued, the road got so bad that in some places it would be incorrect to call it a road. Truckers had stopped and were trying to stop a small portion of the road from collapsing. We being on motorcycles passed without any difficulty. As we rode down, the sun came out and we stopped to soak up the sun. Little did we know it was only light and had very little heat. At the base of the mountain is the very small village of Khoksar, it is the gate way to the district of Lahaul-Spiti in Himachal Pradesh. We stopped at 'Praveen Dhaba' for breakfast and some piping hot tea, it was quarter past six. I do not think there is any edible item that can lift your spirits like a cup of hot tea when temperatures are hovering close at about 10 degrees centigrade. We also realized that we were ridiculously unprepared for the cold and got some new gloves from the village. The very polite and friendly gentleman who ran the place soon made some tea for us and some excellent aloo prathas! We were soon full and on our way, glad and relieved that the 15000 foot Rohtang pass was now behind us. Our goal was to reach Sarchu before night fall. It is only about a 150 kilometres from where we were but we knew it would take us about eight hours. The ride now was very pleasant, the roads were good and the country side was breathtaking! After a while we came across our first serious water crossing, it was not deep at all, but there was quite a bit of water flowing at a good speed and was full of round smooth stones, enough to make one loose traction and fall into the ice cold water. Soon the road turned into a dirt track and we were covered in fine dust and our pace reduced considerably. We soon reached 'Tandi', it took us about an hour to cover the 37 kilometres. Tandi is the only village on the road from Manali up to Leh that has a functioning petrol station. We topped all three motorcycles and took an additional four litres in old mineral water bottles, it is unsafe, but we had no other alternative, if you remember we were unable to get jerry cans. If anyone was to forget filling up at Tandi or did not know that there is no petrol available anywhere along the road, till Leh, will either get stranded or have to buy petrol in black from the many small hotels along the road, who do not hesitate to charge whatever they feel like. About half an hour from Tandi is 'Keylong' and it is the last village where there is a mechanic before reaching Leh and by that I mean somebody who knows to work on a Royal Enfield. Most mechanics refuse to work on them for some reason or the other. We stopped at 'Chuni Auto Works', got the chains on all the motorcycles oiled, as the dust and water had dried them out, got the brakes tested and set off for 'Jispa'. After we left the village and had ridden for a while when we stopped by the road to drink some water and relieve ourselves, noticed a pipe pushed into the side of the mountain and a steady stream of clear water pouring out from it, running down to the road and emptying into the river. We stood and looked at it wondering what its purpose was and then two ladies came up, filled their bottles and then told us that the water is clean and good for drinking. Theoretically, that has to be true, since the water is filtering itself while it is flowing down inside the mountain, so we gave it a shot and found the water to be surprisingly sweet, tasty and cold; we had our fill, filled our now empty bottles and continued on our way. A short while later we suddenly realized that we were again one motorcycle short, we pulled over and waited to regroup, again Akash was the missing rider and we feared he had taken another tumble. We decided to give him another five minutes before we turned around in search of him. However, it was not necessary, just before we turned around to go look for him, we saw him ride up. After he drew abreast to us, we learnt that he had in fact fallen off his motorcycle yet again, apparently there was a pile of very fine loose dust he got caught in and it pulled him down. Anyway, again he was thankfully unhurt and we continued on our way and were soon in Jispa were we stopped for lunch and a short well needed rest. After we had lunch and just as we were setting out, we met a young couple from Delhi who informed us that they were on their way to Sarchu and a bridge about 25 kilometres from Sarchu, at a place called 'Killing Sarai' had washed away and the only way to cross was by going through the river that was fed by melt water and naturally, freezing cold. They advised us to wait till morning and leave before the sun was up so that by the time we reached we would be able to ride across safely because over night the ice would have frozen and reduced the force of the river. The four of us weighed our options and decided we would go anyway and see what the situation is. Killing Sarai is 77 kilometres from Jispa and a good three hours away, it was a gamble we were taking, because if we were unable to cross we would burn up a bunch of fuel, wear out our tyres and ourselves and not reach anywhere (a very bad proposition when you consider that the next petrol station is 270 kilometres away). Before we could reach Sarchu, we had to cross two more tiny settlements/villages; the first is Darcha and the second is Zingzingbar. All foreign tourists are required to register at the police outpost at Darcha, which is at about 11000ft, we reached Darcha pretty quickly, but did not stop and we continued, keeping Sarchu as our destination. We kept our fingers crossed hoping the road was open. We had to deal with numerous water crossings and during one such crossing was where we met the delightful pair of Dr. Lav and Uday. They were two smart young men in a green gypsy who were driving up to Leh from Chandigarh. I stopped them to ask if they had information about the bridge, they answered in the negative and decided to continue just as we had and deal with whatever was the situation. We soon came upon

Zingzingbar; it is a small group of temporary road side settlements, where one can get cheap accommodation and food and is at about 14000 ft. Again, we did not bother to stop in the interest of saving time. To get to the 'alleged' washed away bridge and Sarchu, we had to pass the 'Bara-lacha' pass or Bara-lacha la as it is known, which is in the Zanskar mountain range and it tops off at around 16000 ft. It acts as a water-divide between the Bhaga River and the Yunam River. The higher reaches of the pass was still covered in snow and ice. Legend says that Chandra the daughter of the Moon and Bhaga, son of the Sun God decided to solemnize their celestial marriage by climbing over the pass which also happens to be an ancient trade route. The road up the pass was in very good condition and we made good time. I pulled away from the group as I was by then a little fed up of the cold and just wanted to be done with it and unlike the other guys, dint stop to play in the snow. I soon crested the top and on the way down came across a wall of snow—at least 8 feet high blocking the whole road and a BRO dozer busy clearing the obstruction. BRO is short for the 'Border Roads Organisation'. According to Wikipedia, The Border Roads Organisation (BRO) was formed in 1960 and maintains roads that serve the border areas of India. It is staffed with a combination of Border Roads Engineering Service officers from the General Reserve Engineer Force (GREF) and officers from the Corps of Engineers of the Indian Army. The organisation develops and maintains arterial roads on the borders of India. The BRO operates a network of over 32,885 kilometres of roads and 12,200 metres of permanent bridges. BRO has operations in twenty two states, including the Andaman and Nicobar Islands.

The tunnel I had mentioned earlier being constructed below the Rohtang pass is being excavated by the BRO. I did not get a chance to personally thank anyone, for the kind of work they do in the kind of conditions, it is commendable and extremely difficult. All across the route there are signs put up by the BRO, some of them read, "We gave our today for your tomorrow", that is so true. Back to my story now, I was now waiting for the big bulldozer to clear a path for me, which for it was like cutting butter with a hot knife. In no time I was on my way after honking a thank you to the operator of the dozer. A few minutes after passing the block, I began to feel the front tyre wobble, it was annoying and I thought to myself, 'this is dangerous, I could lose control and fall off the side of the mountain', I stopped and realized that the air pressure in my front tyre was low. I had a slow leak. A slow leak, does not lead to total loss of pressure but the air leaks out at a steady slow pace and the only way to arrest it, is to either stop find the cause and fix it or continue riding, theoretically, the force of the tyre rotating will keep the air in. I quickly pumped in some air and decided to not stop till I could find help. But then a few more kilometres and the tube gave out, I had complete air loss and my front tyre was flat and now dangerously unstable. I pulled over and waited for the other two motorcycles to catch up. However, the gypsy and its two occupants arrived before my companions and they tried to pump air in with their motorised pump, I knew it would not work, because the bead of the tyre was now separated from the rim, or in simple terms the tyre and the rim separated and that would prevent any air from staying in. It is the only time I have ever wished I had tubeless tyres—but I was still hoping against hope that it would work. However, lady luck had different plans for me and my motorcycle. Soon the guys on the gypsy gave up and continued on their way towards the bridge that we believe had been washed away. A little later my companions showed up and we tried fixing it. No luck again, so we decided to limp the motorcycle the remaining twenty eight odd kilometres to Sarchu where I hoped to find help . . . provided the bridge was open. Around the next bend we came upon a GREF camp, the very same camp that had deployed the bulldozer I had crossed a couple of kilometres behind. The camp was bustling with activity, road crews were returning from the various job sites to get some sleep, naturally I figured I would find help there and so walked in to enquire, somehow everybody there seemed the least bit bothered. Either they did not want to have anything to do with me or they did not know anything about fixing a puncture, in spite of there being at least two trucks and a couple of jeeps. Dis-heartened and annoyed I stomped out of the camp and continued to ride towards the bridge, to my great astonishment, it was now repaired and opened to traffic. However, since the bridge was just thrown open to traffic, there was a long line of vehicles on either side waiting to cross over and it was taking time because only one vehicle is allowed on the bridge at a time due to safety concerns. While we waited for our turn, we were greeted by two men who were driving a white 'Mahindra Thar', a beautiful four wheel drive jeep that was perfect for the kind of terrain we were in. Both the men had prior experience driving this route on their motorcycles as well as cars and seeing us on our motorcycles they came over to say hi. I did not ask their names and so shall refer to them as the 'white

Thar guys'. I pointed out our predicament and the two of them immediately offered to help. They too took out their motorised pump and tried to reflate the tyre, in spite of me telling them we had already tried it and failed. Along with them were their wives and a young boy, not more than 5 years old. They then suggested I remove the front tyre and they would take it to Sarchu and get it repaired and the four of us could ride over on two motorcycles and bring it back the next morning, refit it and be on our jolly way. Sounded like an excellent plan and we agreed. Little did we know how awful an idea it was and that he had almost signed our death warrants. Anyway, Anoop and I rode the motorcycle up into the GREF camp and got about removing the tyre. In between all the pulling and tugging, the wives of the white Thar guys came in to use the toilet in the unused rickety shed we were in; they were shortly followed by a wailing child, who wanted to use the toilet. Sounds normal—No! The boy though only 5 years old or lesser by my estimate would not use a dirty toilet and his parents; one of the white Thar guys had given him a medicine to prevent him from going to the toilet. That did not have the desired effect and the boy now was crying to use a toilet. Finally he had his way and all of a sudden we realized that the white Thar guys and their families drove off leaving us with a tyre in our hands. They literally left without saying a goodbye or sorry. We were now in deep trouble. Daylight was fading and a cold wind was blowing hard. Anoop and I quickly put the tyre back on using the torch from our phones for light. Suddenly it was all dark. It took two full hours to remove and put the tyre back on, the whole while Akash and Srikant were waiting by the road in the biting cold made worse by the cold wind. I can assure you that any person not accustomed to such weather will not be able to tolerate the cold. Nothing we could have done would have prepared us for the cold and it finally got to Akash and he refused to move, he said he would not ride another feet and wanted to spend the night at Killing Sarai. I could not help but think of the irony of being found cold and stiff in a place called Killing Sarai! We tried as best as we could to persuade him to leave and come with us to Sarchu where we knew we would find warmth and food, he just refused to move. We could not leave a friend behind, so we all decided to stay back with him and deal with whatever happened. Before I continue let me describe the shed we were sitting in. It was made of thin sheet metal, the doors did not latch and windows were broken. The rear wall of the structure was up to the window in snow and ice. It was cold and it would only get colder as the night progressed. A very scary thought. Inside of me, I knew we would die, if we did not do something about it. My thoughts raced back home to my friends and family to whom I had promised I would make it back in one piece. I thought of my mother, she tried as best as she could to persuade me not to go, I being stubborn and a, 'know it all' brushed aside her fears and threw caution to the wind. Maybe it was the prayers of my beloved ones that got us out! Outside the shed was a small open space, where the vehicles are parked at night. On the other side is a shed used by the road crew. I walked out to the shed of the road crew, it was also a shed similar to the one we were in, but they all had blankets and a fire burning inside the room. I asked if we could also sit in a corner of the room, we would be no trouble and would sleep. They refused out right. I then asked if I could borrow some fuel and wood to build a fire; again they refused, knowing very well that we would not make it through the night without heat. I walked back to my companions and again tried to convince Akash to leave. He refused. It is not like there is any wood lying around the place to make a fire, everything there is wet and damp and there was not a single tree or bush around. We desperately needed to find some source of heat. I'm a big fan of 'Kenneth Anderson', a sixth generation Scotsman and ace hunter and conservationist later on in life. He is best known for hunting down scores of man-eating tigers all over south India's 'Madras Presidency' during the British Raj. I had one of his books with me; I had carried it to read when I had time. I took the book out and set fire to it; it provided us heat for a little while and then died out. A little later we heard a jeep roll into camp. It was the officer of the camp—a Mr. Yadav. He was coming from the GREF camp in Sarchu and headed to Keylong to meet the officer of the GREF camp. We let him know our predicament, he offered all the assistance he could and finally insisted we leave as it was unsafe. He said we could leave my motorcycle and our entire luggage at the camp and go to Sarchu and return the following day and retrieve the motorcycle. He said it would not take more than fifteen minutes to Sarchu and that only the first few kilometres were bad and the rest was as good as a National Highway. With renewed spirits and a convinced Akash we left on two motorcycles for Sarchu. I rode Akash's motorcycle and Anoop and Srikant followed us. The road was beyond bad and was almost completely covered in snow. A little later Akash insisted on riding saying he was feeling better and so we switched places. The ride was slow and long, Mr. Yadav probably said what he did to encourage us to leave the camp and certain death behind. Our only aim was to reach Sarchu and find a nice warm tent to sleep in as there are no permanent structures there, during the summer months temporary shelters pop up to cater to tourists and are gone once winter sets in and the roads are closed to civilian traffic. Akash was leading and after a while the lights of Sarchu showed up in the distance. I could not wait to get out of my wet boots and find a nice cosy bed. A little later the road forked with one going up and the other going slightly down, Akash took the lower road as it seemed nearer to the lights, I too would have probably chosen the same road. That is when we realized we were riding towards a dead end, the road was under construction and ten feet further and we would have plunged to our deaths. Akash got off and I started to ride again, we took the road that was going up, which was actually a detour around the cliff, that we later learnt was actually an under construction bridge. We soon crossed the temporary bridge and were in Sarchu. We stopped at the first tent we saw and got in. It belonged to a Mr Tenzin from Manali. We were greeted by other travellers amongst who were Dr. Lav and Uday. Also with them were a couple and their friend who were on a road trip and driving all the way from Bangalore in south India, up to Leh, via Delhi and Srinagar. The three off them were on their way back to Bangalore and we had all stopped at the same place for the night. They had driven up in a nice military green all-wheel drive Mahindra Thar. I was now convinced that it was the best vehicle to use in such terrain and made up my mind to come again via this road driving a Thar, i.e. if at all I planned to do it again. Our next effort was getting our boots off. Now to most of you it will seem like I'm exaggerating, but for those of you who have been in close to zero degree temperatures; you can vouch for me, when I say that it was so cold that the wet laces of our boots froze solid and it was impossible to get the boots off. We sat by a nice warm stove as our boots thawed and finally were able to get them off. It was so good to be in a warm place. We all had some piping hot black tea. Akash was in the worst condition and everybody in the tent agreed. He was soon fast asleep under a thick quilt. Slowly the other people began to retire to their respective tents and after that I had a nice hot bowl of the famous "Maggie noodles" and also called it a night. It was nine PM. Thus came an end to an extremely long, tiring and cold day. We had been out on the road for more than 18 hours and covered just 230 kilometres. I was glad to be alive and well. I said a silent prayer and was soon out like a blown light bulb. Day four was now officially over and thank God for that.

DAY 5

MAY 27, 2013

We woke up to a hot cup of black tea. It was still cold, so cold that as soon as you got out from under the covers, the cloth would become cold immediately, so cold that it seemed to be wet. It was around eight. We had already decided that we would start only after the sun was up and shining, the 2:30am start of the previous day was not necessary anymore. Unless the weather turned bad, there would be no road restricts all the way, up to Leh. Everybody was still asleep when I looked out. Everything was white, the whitest white I have ever seen. It was then that Mr Tenzin told us a blizzard was blowing in. In a few short minutes the sky was dark and down came the snow; it had apparently snowed the whole night as well. No distinction could be drawn between sky, mountain, road and ground; everything was sparkling white. There was nothing we could do, so everyone turned around and went back to bed. When we awoke again a little later, the blizzard had subsided, everything that was not covered or indoors was blanketed in snow, it was beautiful. Both the motorcycles and all the other cars and jeeps were all covered in snow. Apart from the four of us sharing the room was also two other young men from Manali, they were on their monthly trip to Leh. They were vegetable vendors and used to drive up to Leh in their Mahindra Pick-up, buy fresh vegetables for a bargain and then drive it all the way back to Manali and sell it for a profit. In any other state, this endeavour would have turned out to be a disaster, but here the temperatures are so low all the time that nothing gets spoilt. All the veggies looked like they had been pulled out of the ground an hour ago. Two of the three men are brothers and the third their driver. We began to talk and I asked if they would help us bring my abandoned motorcycle from Killing Sarai to Sarchu. I figured that with all three motorcycles together at one place we would be able to do more from a planning perspective. The younger brother said he would try and talk his brother into helping us. The biggest deterrent for them was fuel. They would be travelling an additional 52 kilometres if they agreed to help us and even the most fuel efficient vehicle will return a bad average in such conditions. I literally begged them and finally got them to agree to help us. It would cost us 4000 rupees to retrieve the motorcycle. We had no choice but to agree, we were the proverbial, "Beggars cannot be Choosers". The cabin of the jeep had room for only three people. We waited for at least one vehicle to come from Killing Sarai before we set off, that would be proof enough that the road was drivable and safe. Two SUVs soon arrived and told us that the road was very difficult to find as everything was white because of the snow. The driver of the jeep was confident we could make it by following the tracks they made and along with the older brother, the driver and I set off from Sarchu to go get my motorcycle. I was hoping it was still there, I knew I had nothing to worry about because the officer of the camp said the motorcycle would be safe, plus nobody in their right mind would want to steal a heavy motorcycle by pushing it in such weather. It took us the better part of an hour to cover the 26 kilometres to Killing Sarai, we had to stop twice to dig the pick-up truck out of the snow drifts and make a path, in the meantime the green Thar had caught up with us and we let them pass. Firstly so that we would not be slowing them down and secondly and more selfishly, so that they would cut a path through the snow and we could follow more easily. It was soon evident that the snow was no issue for them as they effortlessly drove through it, not even stopping once to dig their jeep out of the snow. Soon they pulled away from us and were gone and that is the last we saw of them. The sun was out now and everything was a very bright white. My eyes began to hurt, the driver suggested I put my sunglasses on if I dint want to ruin my eyes. The suggestion sounded absurd, the sun was barely up. He then told me the people here get 'snow blindness', because of not having proper eyewear. I put my sunglasses on, more to amuse him than for my good and it seemed to help. After we reached civilization, I looked it up on the internet and found that it was true! Snow blindness is a condition that is caused by exposure of ultraviolet rays to insufficiently protected eyes. The sun was not only shining down, but the light was reflecting off the snow and ice and magnifying the effect. The driver gloated about that fact that he had not studied beyond the tenth grade but still knew more than I did. Progress was slow till we turned a bend and there was Killing Sarai. My motorcycle would soon be free. All the curses I had rained on her the previous night in frustration and rage were soon forgotten. With great effort the older brother and I pushed the motorcycle out of the camp and down to the main road. It was a phenomenal effort because the air is so rare and the road is in such poor shape. I not being as used to the weather conditions had to stop pushing every few steps to catch my breath. Seeing us, a couple of the people who had refused to help us the previous night came down to give us a hand loading the motorcycle on to the back of the pick-up, I stood back and watched this time, I was in no position to help and would probably just get in the way anyway. The two of them strapped the motorcycle down as I sat up in the cabin away from the cold and snow that had started to fall again! Just as we were getting ready to make the hour long drive back to Sarchu, a white sedan drove up and tried to cross. I remembered seeing the same white car at Sarchu and remembered the people there telling the driver or owner that his car was not made for the current road conditions and he should either turn back or wait for the weather to get better. He obviously ignored their advice and had set out. The driver of the pick-up was mumbling curses under his breath as we watched the car spin out on the ice and in essence polish the road. He was not going anywhere. Finally a couple of people helped him push the car to the side of the road to let us pass. That was the last we saw of the stubborn man and his white car.

As we drove back, I was surprised to see that the terrain had completely changed, it was not white anymore. The few minutes of sun had melted all the snow away and we could see the road as well as the direction in which we were headed. We were soon in Sarchu; we unloaded the motorcycle and set about finding a solution to our predicament. The pick-up was soon ready to leave and the three friendly young men waved us a goodbye and good luck as they drove away smiling. They had made 4000 rupees for two hours' worth of work, who would not be smiling. I however, believe they were smiling because they had helped out a fellow human being in this unforgiving, cold and lonely place. It was around half past eleven in the morning. Our first order of business was to try and see if we could find somebody who would take our motorcycles to Leh, as far as we knew there was no other place we could get the puncture repaired. There was no one there to help us. The problem soon took a turn for the worse when we were told that any truck using the road and heading towards Leh would be so full of supplies, that there would be no place for us to sit, let alone our motorcycles. We needed to change our plan. While I was away retrieving the motorcycle, my companions spoke to a Ukrainian gentleman, he was also on a road trip and had ridden these roads every year for the past ten years. Once the roads are closed, he would go to Goa and have a ball of a time. He did this till he ran out of cash, after which he would head back to Moscow, find employment, make some money and start the whole thing all over again. His name is 'Sananand'. He had seen the motorcycles and walked over from his tent to speak to my companions. He gave us one of the patches he was carrying that could be used to repair the puncture and then proceeded on his way. Since we had this patch with us, we decided that we would try and fix the puncture ourselves. So we set about taking off the tyre, yet again. A little later we saw Sananand ride up towards us, he had decided it was not safe to continue seeing the road conditions and had turned back to Sarchu to wait for the weather to improve. He immediately jumped into the melee to help us. The tyre was taken off easily; the next challenge was taking out the punctured tube. It was going to be an effort since we did not have the right kind of tools for doing such a job. Anyway we started and using pieces of old rusty iron we finally got it out. A quick inspection revealed that the tube had broken off from the valve completely. It was a lost cause. We cursed ourselves for forgetting to get a spare tube. We were now feeling a little stupid for getting ourselves into such a position, I now felt that not going to Jhilmil colony while in Delhi was a bad decision we had made. We had saved about three hours by not going there and now in exchange we ended up losing about 24 hours. A tube was on our list of things to carry, but we had carelessly overlooked it and were now paying the price. The patch Sananand had given us would be of no use either. Dejected we sat down and that is when Mr Tenzin came up to us and handed us an old tube that a previous rider had left behind. We were overjoyed and happy that our luck had finally turned. We tested the tube. Our joy was short lived. This tube too had a small leak right by the valve. This time we decided to try and fix the tube, there was no other alternative available and we decided to give it a shot. For those of you who know how a tube is fixed, you will agree with me when I say that the most effective way of finding the perforation in the tube is by filling it with air and then submerging it in water and check for escaping air by looking for the distinctive tell-tale bubbles. Thankfully that was the only hole. We poured super glue into and let it set; it took about half an hour because it was cold. We then cut a piece of rubber, pushed it over the valve and glued it place and waited for another hour. We then did the uncomfortable task of dipping it in water to check for leaks and to our immense relief there was no air bubbling to the surface. We dried the tube, wrestled it back into the tyre and secured the tyre back in place. After pumping in some air, Anoop rode it up and down the road a few times to test it. All was good. By now it was well past noon. We quickly packed our bags and then came the next delay. Mr Tenzin wanted us to pay three hundred rupees for the tube (a brand new one would be approx. 275 rupees), a tube that was useless to him and anyone else because of the hole in it. He was exploiting the situation, he knew he could ask for more and we would pay him considering the situation. After arguing and cussing for about ten minutes, he finally agreed to let us have it for two hundred rupees. We were in no position to argue, so we paid him the agreed two hundred rupees for it and set off. As per our original plan, we should have left Sarchu by morning and reached Leh—our final destination by late evening. We were way behind schedule and had to make up time. So we decided to ride to the next out post. A place called 'Pang', it is only 79 kilometres from Sarchu, but will take a more than three hours to reach. We left Sarchu and the opportunistic Mr Tenzin behind us and made for Pang, that is more the 15200 feet above sea level. To get to

Pang we would have to ride up and over two mountain passes. Starting the first one by climbing the famous 'Gata Loops', it is about twenty five kilometres from Sarchu and is twenty two hair-pin bends that took us up the mountain side to about 13750 ft. from there on we went up the Nakee La (pass) which topped off at around 15500 ft. and finally the Lachulung La (pass), that topped off at about 16600 ft. Progress was slow, by the time we had crested the Gata Loops and started up the Nakee La pass, day light was fading away into darkness. The only thought going through my mind was the front tyre. I was praying the rudimentary patch holds up. A flat tyre here and the three hour ride would extend well into the night. In all the hurry to leave Sarchu, I had made another critical mistake. I did not pull on the straps and check if the bags that were strapped behind me were secured to the motorcycle properly and soon it began to slide towards the right. It was uncomfortable and dangerous as it kept pulling the motorcycle towards the side it was leaning off and that unfortunately happened to be the side where the mountain fell off into darkness below. I stopped twice to readjust the bag, but the biting cold had made my hands close to unusable. So I heaved it onto the motorcycle and continued till I had to stop to do it again. At one point the pulling was so strong that I could not turn and rode the motorcycle off the road and up the mountain side. I thanked God that I was turning towards the mountain and was riding pretty slowly. The motorcycle was heavy with all the bags and I could not get it back onto the road myself and waited for the others to catch up. Once they reached, they helped me back out on to the road and we were on our way. It started getting increasingly colder and soon the water on the road was starting to freeze over and that made the descend even more treacherous. At places I had to stop and stamp a path out through the thin layer of ice. Using the brakes was out of the option because the roads were slick. We were controlling the speed of our descend using the gears and finally were off the mountains. We had a few more kilometres to ride before we could shut down for the day. Akash was now in the lead and I was following close behind him, not more than ten feet away. We reached the last turn that would take us off the mountain and as I was making the turn the unstable bag took the opportunity to take a bow and took me down along with it. Everything was happening in slow motion, I could feel the center of gravity shifting and knew I was going down and instinctively lifted my leg and stepped away from the motorcycle and watched as it leaned on to its side. Akash did not see or hear a thing and kept riding on. I figured he would at least notice my headlight fading away, considering that everything else around us was shrouded in complete darkness. The saddle bags that hung over each side and the custom fitted rear crash guard prevented the motorcycle from actually making any contact with the ground. The engine shut off and I was standing surrounded by deathly silence, it was a very unsettling feeling. The only thing that prevented me from screaming like a little girl was the bright white light from my motorcycles' headlamp piercing the darkness straight ahead of me. I looked around me and could see nothing. I could not hear a bird or any other sound that a city dweller is so accustomed to hearing. I did not wait for another second; I quickly picked up the motorcycle, started it and took off from there as fast as I safely dared too, not even bothering to re adjust the bag that had caused the whole debacle. I could see the headlight from Akashs' motorcycle bobbing up and down far away in the distance. After another half an hour of riding, I saw the welcoming lights of Pang. As I drew closer, Akash was speaking to an elderly gentleman. He was the owner of the tent in front of which the two of them were having their conversation. As I pulled up to him, I asked him to enquire about a place to stay. It would cost 150 rupees a person per night, apart from food and anything else we used. We did not wait any longer, we got off our motorcycles and made a bee line for the tent. We dumped our bags in a corner and did not even bother to change our clothes. But before we could stretch out on to the comfortable mattresses, we had to deal with frozen shoelaces yet again before we could get our boots off. The old man was helped by his wife and a young lady, who we believe is their daughter. They were the nicest people we met on the whole trip, genuine, kind hearted and very friendly. That being said, we never encountered a rude person anywhere along those desolate roads. Ten minutes away from the tent was an Indian Army camp, the only place in the area that had a telephone and a doctor along the whole stretch, starting from Jispa up to Pang. None of our cell phones had worked since we left Jispa the day before and we were sure that our families would have been worried sick. We were all too tired to go make a call, so we wolfed down a scrumptious meal of Roti's with potato and cauliflower curry, a double omelette each and all of this was washed down with lots of sweet, hot lemon tea. It was half past eight. We had covered a distance of 79 kilometres in four hours. The least we had ridden on any day throughout the whole trip, but nobody cared. We were closer to our final destination and had the formidable Tunglung La (pass) ahead of us. Dog tired that we were, all of us were fast asleep within a few minutes of hitting the bed. Day 5 was over and behind us.

DAY 6

MAY 28, 2013

The sun was well up over the horizon when we woke up. Since Sarchu did not have a toilet, I had not done my business and that was next on my agenda. I soon learnt that each tent did not have a toilet, but they all together have a communal toilet that was constructed by the army, it did not have a running water supply. I took a bottle of warm water from the gentleman who owned the tent, crossed the road and walked over towards the funny looking structure. It was almost two stories tall. You will understand what I mean by 'almost' in a few minutes. I would strongly urge my squeamish readers to skip the next two sentences. The actual toilet is on the upper floor of the structure. I walked up a small flight of stairs to it, pushed open a door and found all the necessities of a toilet absent, there was no toilet bowl, no tap, the window was just a hole and I had to hold the door with my hands to keep some else from

41

walking in on me while I did my business. There was an open hole in the floor, out of curiosity I peeped down the hole; I was not the first person to use that toilet that day, there was a small steaming pile of evidence on the lower floor, if I may say so. There is an opening on the lower floor from where the waste would be scooped out and disposed of. I really think the five rupees I paid to use it is not enough. Nobody will learn the value of a toilet till they are presented with such a situation. I'm not a squeamish person and I have ridden lonely, sparsely populated roads many times before and expect such things, I'm of the breed that considers the 'world to be my toilet', when I have to go. Now that, that was done I walked back and decided to fire up my cold, dirty motorcycle. I again got some boiling water to pour over the engine and she started right up without any fuss. I quickly did a walk around to make sure everything was still in place and no nuts or bolts had worked themselves loose from the constant jostling and bouncing. I was also looking for cracks in the frame, because the cold can make steel and metal brittle and the bouncing may lead to fatigue cracks, which can be a major problem. During the walk around, I realized my front tyre pressure was low and so pumped some air into and then rode towards the army camp to check if there was somebody there who know how to fix our puncture, it was a natural thought considering the large amount of vehicles they have, both big and small. Unfortunately, we found no help there, so we packed up, paid the extremely kind family and set off to conquer Tanglang La and reach Leh. The only thing we did different when we started riding was have Anoop sit pillion this time round as he was unwell from something he had eaten the previous night. It was a calculated risk we were taking. The roads would certainly get dangerous, but it made more sense to let Anoop sit this one out because passing out while crossing Tanglang La would be a bad thing. It would also be a baptism by fire for Srikant. Within minutes of starting we started to climb again and once we finished the climb we were presented with the best football ground in the world. We were on the awe inspiring 'More Plains' or 'Morey Plains'. It is forty kilometres and at about 13000ft. As we rode deeper into the plains, the grandeur of nature and the insignificance that we are as humans became alarmingly clear. If you stand anywhere in the middle of these plains, you will wonder how humans managed to tame it. Either side of the road is just vast, empty expanses, not a single tree or animal. After a while, there is just a straight black road ahead and it is the same in the rear view mirror. It makes you feel very lonely, vulnerable and exposed. The road soon began to turn to gravel and then gave out to a mud road. When the roads around these places turn bad, it is a precursor of bad things to come. We were soon going to start climbing the infamous 'Tanglang La'. The climb was slow and very difficult; the road was almost non-existent and very slick around the bends. To add to it, we had to deal with loaded fuel tankers on their way down to re-supply the camps in Pang and further south. The roads were in a pretty bad state of repair. I slowed down to a crawl and said a silent prayer. The cold soon got bad and to my horror, it started to snow. I was now torn between turning back, going forward or stopping and enjoying the snow fall. Better judgement prevailed in the end and I pushed on. However, I still could not keep my focus and kept looking down at my jacket to see the pretty little flakes of snow strike it. I knew very well that losing focus for even a minute is dangerous, but the snow was so enchanting, I looked up every now and then and suddenly realized that I had reached the edge of the road sooner than I calculated and had to literally slam on the breaks to keep myself from riding off the mountain side. That drove the point home and I was more focused than ever. I reached the top and stopped for about a minute to take in the view. There was nothing there but silence, if the howling wind was ignored. I started descending and came upon a very small tent by the road and a lady sitting by a fire making some tea. The fire was fuelled by donkey dung, which reinforced the fact that we were in a cold arid desert that barely had any vegetation at any time of year. The fire looked very welcoming and I had to stop. The lady was very surprised to see me and flashed a wide, ear to ear smile; I tore off my gloves and literally put my hand into the fire. Again the lady who had no gloves at all was very surprised and she rubbed my hands together with hers to warm them up and offered me some hot tea. As I sat there speaking to her, a man came out of the tent, he was even more surprised than the lady. He took one look at my motorcycle and told me that we were too early for the season. We were the first set of the bikers to come by this year. He was the person in charge of a hand full of people who were working on the road, I inquired about the road ahead and I sat a few more minutes and then continued with my descend. The road was bad for the next ten minutes and then was the best road I had seen in the past two hours. I was so excited and opened up the throttle and thundered down the mountain, definitely faster than recommended. I was at the bottom and nine kilometres from Rumtse in no time. It is then that I realized that I had left the others behind in my hurry to get down. I looked for a safe place to pull over and wait for the other two motorcycles to catch. Most of you probably think that it should be easy to find a safe place to stop, but more than half the stretch is constantly under the threat of landslides and now that I was at the bottom, the threat was greater, coupled with the approaching summer and melting snow and ice. I soon came upon a small bridge that was closed on either side by a small stone wall. Vehicular traffic had to manoeuvre off the road, drive through the river and get back on the road on the other side of the bridge. I was in no mood to ride through another cold river and looked at a small gap on either side of the wall blocking the road. It looked safe enough to me and I rode through and over the bridge to the other side. The road on the other side of the bridge looked safe enough to stop so I pulled over to the side and waited, using this time to stretch my legs. In about ten minutes Akash reached and we waited together and then Akash took off saying he could not bear the cold any longer and would wait for us in Rumtse, which was now about seven kilometres away. I continued waiting and after a few minutes walked towards the bridge to see why it was closed. I walked up and down the length of the bridge and soon saw that the bridge had been lifted off its supports by the ice and was therefore unsafe for heavy vehicle traffic. Twenty minutes after I stopped Srikant and Anoop came down. I was relieved to see them. We decided to take in the beauty for a few minutes and then pushed on to Rumtse. By the time we reached Rumtse, Akash had already found a phone booth. We all took turns to call home. It was our first chance to call home since we left Manali on May 26. Our next destination was Upshi, forty six kilometres from Leh. The roads were excellent, at least for a two wheeler. On the way we met a couple we had met at Sarchu, somewhere along the road their SUV struck a stone or some other hard object that was jutting out of the road surface and it tore a hole in the oil sump and since the vehicle was full of sensors and computers it simply shut itself down when it ran out of oil and this happened in the middle of nowhere, luckily for them a passing army truck offered to take them till Upshi, where they spent the night. We met them when they had come back with a mechanic to try and fix the damage. We wished them luck and continued on our way. In about half an hour of meeting the couple we came across a board put up by the state welcoming us to Leh. As far as we were concerned we had reached our goal, even if it was not the actual town. We stopped, took a few pictures and continued on towards Leh. The weather was very plesant and we were throughly enjoying ourselves. The scenery was breath taking and everything looked very clean and fresh. As we were nearing Leh we came up on a huge army installation, it was home to the 'Trishul Eagles' a division of the Indian Army. What stood out most as we crossed the army facilities was a huge Trishul that was on top of a mountain behind the base. It is a type if trident, and means 'Three Spear" in Sanskrit. A little while later we crossed the Indus River and were on the outskirts of Leh by 4:00PM. Being a place frequented by motorcyclists we soon found a Royal Enfield Specialist and stopped and got the front tube of my motorcycle swapped out for a brand new one and this time it was done by a man who made his living doing this. We also got two extra tubes; certainly did not want a repeat of what happened at Sarchu. Half an hour later we were in Leh.

Leh is the former capital of the Kingdom of Ladhak. Now it is a district in the state of Jammu and Kashmir, the northern most state in India. It is at about 11500 feet and has the highest airport in India and amongst the highest airports in the world. As soon as you enter the town the one thing that jumps out is the ruined Leh Palace, former mansion of the royal family of Ladhak. Leh was an important stop over for the trade routes between the Indus valley, Tibet, Kashmir and China. We were euphoric and could not contain our excitement. We checked into a hotel had a nice hot shower and I climbed under the covers while the others went out to explore. We had a nice hot dinner and were soon fast asleep. We had ridden about 180 kilometres in about six hours.

We had finally reached our destination. We had ridden more 1000 kilometres in six days, including the one day we lost because of my flat tyre and the blizzard. We had reached the halfway point of the journey.

DAY 7

MAY 29, 2013

Our rooms had a gorgeous view. We could see the snow-capped mountains far off and it was the most beautiful view from any hotel I have ever stayed in. I woke up when I saw a little light outside, Srikant; with who I was sharing the room was fast asleep. It took me a couple of minutes to realize that it was a false dawn. A 'false dawn', is a curious phenomenon that is heralded by a momentary light, but within a few minutes a pall of darkness once again envelopes the land, till a wider spreading glow in the eastern sky, perhaps twenty minutes later announces the true dawn and the beginning of another day. Until very recently I had no clue about this strange phenomenon. It is a roughly triangular glow that is seen in the night sky that appears to come in almost the same area from where the sun would rise. It is apparently caused by sunlight scattered on space dust. Now you may wonder why you have never seen it when you were at home. Well, the reason is, that the light is so delicate, if I may say so, that even a little pollution or moonlight can render it invisible. Leh, being so fresh and the very little amount of pollution was the reason it was visible. I have read about it many times, but this was the first time I was actually seeing it and probably the last time considering the direction in which the quality of the air and the environment is going in the other cities in India. I woke up again by eight and we were all soon ready to start exploring Leh. We had originally planned to spend two days in Leh, but unfortunately because of the day we lost we had to cut our stay down to one day. There was a long list of places we wanted to visit, but now that list would have to be cut short. We looked at all the places we wanted to visit and our list boiled down to the famous 'Pangong Lake' and 'Khardung La'. We looked at many different factors before we finally froze on Khardung La. The biggest factor that tilted the balance in Khardung La's favour was the distance. Khardung La is a mere 49 kilometres, which would take us about 2 hours one way and Pangong Lake is 185 kilometres which would take us upwards of 5 hours or more one way. With that dilemma behind us we went looking for a place for breakfast. Being a tourist destination, there are many little restaurants and small hotels where any kind of cuisine is readily available and it is fairly affordable too. We had a nice English breakfast of cheese omelettes, hash brown potatoes and toast, all washed down with freshly squeezed fruit juice. During the pre-trip walk around I had noticed the engine oil was lower than I would like it. Royal Enfield's have a nasty habit of literally eating the oil when ridden for long distances continuously. We again did not think of getting extra oil, even though we were aware of this problem. I walked up to a gentleman who ran a bike rental shop and asked him from where I could get some oil. I also noticed a nasty dent on the exhaust pipe. I am assuming I hit a stone or something sticking out of the road somewhere between Pang and Leh at least that is what I believe happened. Before I could get the oil topped up, we headed to the District Collectors office to get the permits that we require if we need to go up to Khardung La. The permit costs one hundred each and there is also an environment protection fee of two hundred a person. The fee I believe is used to clear up the debris that tourists leave behind after their visit. Plastic/disposable bags are banned in Leh and in most places mineral water bottles are not allowed to be carried away from the restaurant, but still the mountain side is littered with garbage. Most hotels will get the permits for you if you pay them a little extra. We decided to do this ourselves; all we needed was identity proof, vehicle registration papers and copies of it. While the others were busy getting it done, I went to buy some oil. By the time I was done, the permits were procured and we started towards Khardung La. The climb starts even before we leave town and the road is in exceptionally good condition. We expected to reach the top within an hour and a half. The weather was pleasant and we were thoroughly enjoying ourselves. At about 13000 feet we came up on a sign board that said 'Leh View Point', it gives a spectacular view of the whole town and is something that I will not forget in a while. We then reached 'South Pullu', it is a police camp and the army check post, fourteen kilometres from the top. There is a board at the check post suggesting tourists do not spend more than thirty minutes at the top because we gain about 7000 feet in less than two hours. Every vehicle going up has to stop and show their permits and if for some reason a tourist is not aware of this requirement there is nothing they can do other than turn around, go back to town, get the permits. We got our permits checked, left a copy of it with the personnel and continued. The road condition began to deteriorate almost immediately beyond the check post and was soon a wide dirt track. The traffic was pretty heavy with tourists coming down from the pass as well as trucks and buses coming from the village of Khardung in the Nubra valley, which is beyond Khardung La. Our permits would allow us to ride up to Khardung La only. We saw considerable amount of road work along the way being done by the BRO and the army. Two and a half kilometres from the top, we were stopped by a road crew. They were methodically and systematically pulling down the mountain side. It was being done to control landslides; a pre-emptive strike. We were asked to shut off our motorcycles and wait for at least fifteen minutes while the road was cleared of the boulders that had already been pulled down from the mountain side. Traffic was backing up on both sides so the crews were working as fast as they safely could. There were two bulldozers and a third one that had a hydraulic hammer instead of a scoop. I got off my motorcycle and walked up to one of the men and started talking to him. My first question was, if they kept pushing the boulders down, would it not go and land on the road below, then giving them the next task of going there and pushing it down again. He was very confident, when he told me that all the snow that is on the mountain side would retard the motion of the boulder and stop it dead in its tracks. Some of these boulders were the size of a small family car. As we stood watching the boulders tumbling down the mountain side, I noticed a particularly large boulder was not stopping or even slowing down for that matter. I pointed it out to the person I was talking to, he was still confident it would stop, but the boulder kept picking up speed, till it finally stopped rolling and start bouncing down the mountain side. It was by now so far down the mountain side, we could no longer hear it, but the distinctive sparks that come when rock strikes rock was clearly visible in the dim morning light. It was at least a thousand feet below us and as it was approaching the road below, we saw two SUV's approach it; a white one and a black one. We could not clearly identify the make of the vehicles, but instinctively started yelling to the drivers at the top of our voices. The Black SUV which was trailing the white one suddenly picked up speed and passed the white one, a move that no normal person would have made on such a road. We assume he saw the boulder bouncing down the mountain side. Then like in the movies, everything seemed to happen in slow motion, it seemed to take forever for the boulder to complete its last revolution, but in fact it was probably just two seconds because the boulder impacted the white SUV between the 'A' pillar and the front right side wheel, the impact was hard enough to push the vehicle off the road and on to the shoulder. The man and I both stood with our hands on our heads and looked for some sort of activity around the vehicle, soon people came out and everybody looked fine, but we were a thousand feet above them and did not know for sure. The man ran up to the bulldozer and stopped the work and everybody stepped out towards the edge of the road to see what happened. Inside, I knew that we were going to be there for a while. Two days before our arrival to Leh, the pass was closed because of heavy snowfall, it was still biting cold and we now had no clue for how long we would have to wait, just a mere two and a half kilometres from our goal. We contemplated walking, but since the air is so rare, it would take a huge effort to walk that distance. To give you a perspective of how taxing it is on the body; doing anything, maybe something as simple as lifting bags or walking uphill for ten minutes, will make you feel like you were running for about an hour and then it will take at least another ten minutes of concentrated breathing to bring it back to normal. While we waited, a small stone, about the size of a golf ball rolled off the mountain and fell on the instrument cluster of my motorcycle, it was lights off for the speedometer, tachometer, odometer, fuel gauge and RPM meter, sadly the needles did not move again till the motorcycle was transported back to Hyderabad and the whole cluster swapped out for a new one. One small stone cost me quite a bit of money, but I'm still thankful it was not like the one that took out the cab, because if it was, it would have been lights out for me and you would not be reading this book. We had by now waited for about fifteen minutes and other vehicles, all cabs, had caught up with us and now there was a long line of cars and our three motorcycles waiting for the road to re-open. The four of us set a deadline; we would wait another fifteen minutes and turn around. It would have been a crushing defeat for us to have come so far and then have to turn back so close of our goal. Ten minutes later we saw a short man in army uniform walk up and start yelling at the crew to clear the road. It was the Commanding Officer from the army camp at Khardung La. Apparently it is not safe from a national security perspective if traffic backs up at the pass for too long. He instructed the vehicles from the top be let down before any vehicles are allowed up. The bulldozers took up a whole side of the road and we were asked to squeeze in behind them. As soon as the road was open, Anoop shot through the gap paying no heed to the road crew desperately trying to control the traffic, I did not wait for another second, I took off behind him and Akash followed me. We snaked through the backed up traffic and in fifteen minutes we were at the top of the pass. We had conquered the highest motorable road in the world and there is a board at the top that mentions it as well. We were standing 18380 feet above sea level. The height of the pass is a topic of great dispute and many independent researchers as well travellers have proven the pass to be lower than claimed. I however, could not check myself because my phone was out of network coverage area and therefore the GPS was not working. There is apparently another road that is a higher than Khardung La, but it is probably not publicized so much or as well-known because the access to the road is restricted to the Indian Army. There may be other roads as well, but they may not be motorable in the true sense. So, Khardung La is the highest motorable road that is open to civilian traffic and I'm going to stick to the figure that was on the board till they change the board, any way, it will still be higher than most people will ever go in their life time. From the top of the pass the road continues on to the Nubra valley, where we did not have the time or a permit to go to. At the top is a cafeteria, called the

'Rinchen Cafeteria', it is the world's highest functioning cafeteria. Unfortunately it was closed the day we were there because of the blizzard that hit the pass two days before we had reached. Khardung La is under the control of the Siachen Brigade and there is an army outpost at the top. People who say that soldiers are rude and grumpy must not have met the soldiers we met at the top. They were extremely friendly and were always smiling. During the initial stages of planning we thought it would be fun to be able to take photo of the four of us at the top of the pass wearing a 'Kasavu Mundu' or brocaded dhoti, traditional attire that men in Kerala wear for festive occasions; to put what it looked like into words would be to say, that it is basically like a wraparound skirt (without the string to tie it up) with colourful borders, with the more festive ones having borders of gold. We all packed one each and even carried it up to the pass, but it was so cold that we dropped the idea of taking pictures wearing it, even before we made it to the top. We spoke to a few of the soldiers, walked around for a few minutes, took in a deep breath of the fresh, albeit a little thin air, took lots of photographs and then started descending. The memory of the boulder that whacked the SUV was still fresh in my mind, so all the way down, I kept looking up at the mountain side to see if anything was rolling down towards me. I for sure would not have any sort of protection like the people in the SUV had; my helmet would be crushed in like an egg-shell. Thankfully nothing untoward happened. The sun had been out for a little while now and the road was beginning to get slick and slippery, one wrong move or a small error in judging the braking distance would be enough to send one over the edge and there was plenty of evidence to prove how treacherous the road is. The mountain side was littered with old rusty wrecks, most of them just empty shells, everything that is of any value had long since been salvaged or stolen. A little while later we came across the wrecked SUV or rather a Multi-utility vehicle. It was a Toyota Qualis, which was running tourists up and down the pass. The Commanding Officer, who had about an hour ago ordered for the road to be cleared, was now standing beside the wreck with a few of the road crew from the BRO. The vehicle was a total loss, it looked like a juice carton that had a side stamped in. Beside the vehicle was the boulder and it was the size of a small car, I stopped and walked over to the wreck, it looked pretty bad, the steering column was all crushed into the cabin. The officer was standing behind the wreck and told me that none of the tourists were hurt; the driver however, was badly shaken and had a bruised leg. He was also ecstatic that the boulder did not have enough of room to build more momentum, because another five more feet and the vehicle would have rolled over the edge, seriously injuring everyone on board if not killing them. He finally asked us to leave because there was still a very real possibility of more boulders rolling down the hill and we were directly in the slide path. We continued on down, stopping every now and then to take pictures and in another hour were back in Leh. It was half past four in the evening and we knew it would not get dark till at least 7:30PM. Once we were back in town Anoop, Srikant and Akash went to get the motorcycles checked and I headed back to the hotel. The three of them returned within the hour. While they were getting their motorcycle's checked over, they met Uday and Dr. Lav, who were surprised to see us. The two of them had been to Leh many times before by car as well as motorcycle and were pretty well acquainted with the town. They invited us to dinner and we could not say no; rather did not want to say no, it would be a great opportunity to see the night life in Leh. We decided to meet up at 8:30PM. We were planning to leave Leh, early the next morning, so we quickly did a little shopping, things are relatively cheap, but almost everything being sold was something that can only be used in cold places none the less we got some stuff to bring back home. We kept the things in our hotel room and went to meet Uday and Dr. Lav, we exchanged stories and laughed about the many funny things that had happened along the way, it was a welcoming change to meet and talk to different people after spending almost seven days talking to the same people. Uday is a part of the three member team that drove more than 4000 kilometres from Kanyakumari in the south to Leh in the north in a record 79.5 hours. There was a nice warm fire blazing, around which we were sitting having dinner. The sky was clear and the stars looked like millions of little diamonds, I watched the smoke curl up from the fire and disappear in the flickering, fitful radiance from the comforting warmth of the fire. It was soon well past eleven and time to get some sleep; we had a long ride ahead of us the next day. We sought our farewells and headed back to our hotel. I made sure to pack my bags before I slept, and sleep well we did. Day seven ended on a high note, with a new found respect for nature and the mountains. The beauty of these places make people forget how dangerous they can be. Two weeks after we left Leh, a couple was being driven up the road to Khardung La in a cab when the driver supposedly lost control and the car plunged off the mountain side, killing the couple and their driver. The saddest part of it was that the couple's grown up children were following in a second car and saw it all happen. What caused the accident to happen remains a mystery.

DAY 8

MAY 30, 2013

We planned to be up and out of Leh latest by 5:30AM, but when we finally woke it was eight in the morning. There were many reasons we wanted to leave early. The most compelling reason was that the day we reached Leh, the Srinagar-Leh highway was closed because of landslides. We knew for sure the road being a very busy highway would be opened in as little as three or four hours, the second, and to be honest the only other reason, was to try and make it to Srinagar the same day. It is almost 420 kilometres from Leh to Srinagar and the longest distances we had ridden on any given day so far was 300 and that too on plain, flat, well paved roads. We still hoped we would make it. We hurriedly got ready and set to doing the now annoying task of tying down the bags on the motorcycle. If it was not done correctly the first time, we would have to keep stopping to readjust the bag—an unwanted waste of time. The hotel bills settled we were out and on our way in record time. It took a mere thirty minutes from the time we woke up, to the time we started to move. We decided to get out of town, before we stopped to have breakfast. We stopped at the only petrol station in Leh, topped up the tanks and we were off on our return journey. It would not take as much time as it did to reach Leh, because the roads were much better and we only had a two high passes to clear before reaching low altitudes. The road is National Highway 1 and stretches from Srinagar all the way up to Leh. The landslides that had happened a few days back was still fresh in my mind and I instinctively kept looking up when riding past mountains. The road is just as treacherous as the road we took to reach Leh, but since it was so busy, we felt safe. It follows the historic trade route that runs along the Indus River; it presented us with a breath taking view of villages that had lots of cultural influence. It is also the highway that was used to mobilize the Indian Army during the Kargil war in 1999. The sun was high up in the sky and a pleasant cool wind was blowing. There was lots of traffic, cars as well as petroleum tankers. We soon reached the legendary 'Magnetic Hill'; the reason this point was so famous was the fact the any car left in neutral would roll up the slight incline without any power. What it is, in fact is that the layout of the surrounding land produces an optical illusion that plays tricks on the gullible human mind; it makes a very slight downhill slope appear to be an uphill slope and the biggest contributor to the success of the illusion is the completely obscured horizon, without a reference point, it is easy to mistake a downhill slope for an uphill slope, so naturally, a car left in neutral will seem like it is going uphill, when it is actually going downhill. I am sure that if there was a tree or some other structure on the ground, the illusion would not have worked. Akash and I did not bother to stop and powered on down the hill. Anoop and Srikant, however, did stop for photographs. The mountains soon gave out to lush green fields. Maybe it was all the thin air, but the green there looked greener than in south. We stopped for breakfast at a hotel right beside the road. The whole area was enveloped in pure serenity. Traffic was not too thick, just the occasional bus and cab. We had Maggie noodles, dim sums and piping hot cups of tea. We sat for a little while longer and then continued on our way, we soon began to climb the first of the two mountains between Leh and Srinagar that we knew were going to take time. There are actually more than two, but as far as we were concerned, there were only two of them that would be a challenge. After having ridden over, Rohtang, Baralacha La and Tanglung La, nothing was a challenge anymore, the roads headed south were heavenly and the risk of falling rocks and boulders are not an ever present danger. This pass is also a part of the Zanskar Mountain range. About a hundred and twenty kilometres outside Leh is Lamayuru. Lamayuru is best known for its tenth century 'Gompa' as well as the famous 'Moonland', as the locals referred to it. When you see the golden yellow formations on the granite hills, it becomes very clear why it was called so. The view is mesmerizing; it is something that I cannot describe and neither can I compare it with anything I have ever seen, all I can say is that it looks very alien and different. The landscape is a result of erosion of lakebed deposits of a glacial lake that used to exist here. People believe that during the

Buddhist scholar Naropa's time the lake drained out through cracks in the hills. Unfortunately time was something we did not have much to spare, so we kept riding and soon reached the first of the mountains in our path. The pass is called 'Fotu La' and tops of at 13400 ft. By this point of time, we had been riding for so long that, it felt awkward when we were not sitting on the motorcycles, time quickly went by and we were soon riding up towards the next pass. This one is the 'Namika La' also a small relatively low pass, topping of at about 12000 ft. We still had that second challenging mountain to conquer. The next major town would be Kargil. After a few hours of sustained riding, we realized that trying to reach Srinagar would not be possible, and not only that it could be dangerous as well. The whole length of the highway is dotted with many small villages and finding accommodation is easy, but there are spans that do not have any sort of shelter for long distances and we did not want to get caught in one of these stretches, so we decided we would halt at 'Drass', sixty kilometres after Kargil. The ride was uneventful, till I felt a very familiar wobble in the front tyre again, I was losing air, the last time I felt this was in Baralach La and at that time I was leading the group, so I had nothing to worry about, at least I would not be left behind. But this time I was trailing, I was the last motorcycle and the others were not in sight. Finally all the air went out and it was difficult to control the motorcycle, I stopped by the side and asked, if there was a shop I could get it fixed at, thankfully there was one, but nobody knew how far away it was. Considering that the place I was approaching was a village, it could not be too far, a maximum of five kilometres, so I kept riding, knowing very well that I could further damage the tube or even the rim. A little further I came up on Anoop, Akash and Srikant. They were waiting for me to catch up. We soon found a shop and the mechanic had no clue how to remove the wheel, he had never worked on a Royal Enfield. We helped him take it off, he replaced the tube with a new one we gave him and patched up the old one for us. I was curious to know why this tube also got punctured, there was no nail or other foreign object embedded in the tyre. The mechanic, then told us that the person who had put in the tube the previous time, the professional in Leh, had done it incorrectly. The tube was not put in straight and over time, the twisted parts of the tube rubbed together and finally tore a hole in the place where the two parts were touching. We paid the man the forty rupees he asked for and continued. It was the second puncture my motorcycle had suffered. It cost us a considerable amount of time altogether, but thankfully that was the only trouble the vehicles gave us throughout the trip. The Royal Enfield's were living up to their reputation of being strong and reliable. We reached Kargil by around 4:00PM. It is a small, very beautiful town, second largest town in Ladhak after Leh. It is at a relatively low altitude of about 8000 ft. and the Indus River runs along the side of the town. This town is better known for the Kargil war that took place in this sector, the war started because of infiltration by the Pakistani army as well as militants over the Line of Control and into Indian Territory. We did not stop and decided to push on till Drass and have a late lunch there. As we were leaving town we came upon a huge boulder lying smack in the middle of the road and a bulldozer trying to push it off, over the side and into the raging Indus River below. The boulder was big and it took a little time for it to be cleared. In about ten minutes we were on our way. The road was in good condition over all, but then it was interspersed with roads that were so bad, that we had to stop, back up and find another gap to ride through the huge pot holes. I was later told that the parts of the road in disrepair are actually not neglected, but intentionally not repaired. I was curious, now why would the BRO leave sections of road all muddy and messy, while the rest were in excellent condition. For the curious of my readers, it is because of the constant landslides. When I come to think about it, almost all the sections of bad roads we encountered from the day we started from Manali were in bad condition because these stretches were prone to landslides. It made no sense of the BRO to fix it up and then have to re-do it, when the next landslide damages it again. Now that summer was approaching and the ice was melting, landslides were occurring more frequently. Drass is 60 kilometres from Kargil and we reached in about one and a half hours. Drass is often referred to as the 'Gateway to Ladhak'; it shot to prominence in 1999 when the war started. Drass in the local dialect means "Hell". Drass would be the second place we crossed with a name that scared the life out of me, the first being 'Rohtang pass'. Just before we entered Drass was a board that welcomed us to the second coldest inhabited place in the world. The lowest recorded temperature in Drass was a bone chilling minus 50 degrees centigrade. Just as we were entering Drass, we came across the famous 'Draupadi kund', according to legend, Draupadi the tragic female protagonist of the Hindu epic, the 'Mahabharata', took her final bath here before her death in the Himalayas. Another ten kilometres later we reached the 'Kargil War Memorial', we had to stop here irrespective of our time constrains. It is also called the Bimbat War Memorial and is the prime attraction of Drass. The memorial is located about 5 km from the town across the Tiger Hill and it was built in honour of the brave soldiers who died in the Kargil war. A poem by Harivansh Rai Bachchan, father of veteran Bollywood actor, Amitabh Bachchan, is inscribed on the gateway of the memorial. The names of the soldiers who lost their lives in the war are inscribed on the Memorial Wall. A museum is also a part of the memorial; it houses pictures of Indian soldiers, archives of important war documents and recordings, Pakistani gear and weapons, and official emblems of the Army from the Kargil war. 'Operation Vijay', ('Victory' in Hindi), was the name given to the operation to clear Kargil of enemy soldiers. It is a place that is very emotionally charged. Once you enter, the gates is a tarred road that leads up to the memorial, where a solider in full combat gear minus his weapon will tell you all that happened during the war. If there was an option to join the army there, I would have signed up for sure. Suddenly the oath an officer of the army takes is just not words anymore. *"The Safety, Honour and Welfare of your country comes first, always and every time / The Honour, Welfare and Comfort of the men you command comes next / Your own Ease, Comfort and Safety comes last, always and every time."* All the pictures and stories that are there to see and be heard will make any person patriotic. It was very touching and there were many other visitors who had tears in their eyes. I was honoured and humbled to be able to stand in the midst of these men, past and present, alive and dead. There is a small souvenir shop, from where I purchased a key ring for my motorcycles' key and a pack of postcards. There is also a cafeteria where scrumptious vegetarian food is sold at very reasonable prices. We had not had anything to eat since breakfast and the sight of food, made us want to have some. The food we purchased was finished in a flash. As a rule we tried to avoid riding after the sun went down, because the roads were dangerous and we were not familiar with the terrain or traffic. It was beginning to get dark when we finally set out to Drass and in about fifteen minutes we reached. As expected, Drass is a small town that had one main road that ran right through the middle. It was a very pretty sight in the fading light. We looked for a place to stay and the first hotel we saw was run by the Jammu & Kashmir tourism board. The prices were reasonable, we could all share one room and would cost us only seven hundred and fifty rupees a night—benefits of government run accommodation. We parked our motorcycles, undid our bags and carried it in. Then we saw the down side of it, the room was amongst the dirtiest rooms I have ever slept in, let alone during the trip! The floors were carpeted; most people will consider this a luxury, including me. These carpets however, were filthy as can be. There were huge stains on it and I do not think it had been cleaned since it was put in. The walls were stained red, not with blood . . . it was beetlenut, which somebody had chewed and spat out. The wiring was all exposed. The fourth person would have to sleep on the floor and we got an extra mattress, along with a blanket and a quilt. The quilt was so dirty that we could barely see any of the original pink colour in some places, only black and brown. The bathroom was old, with cracked tiles on the floor and no hot water; because the heater was broken (We preferred not to have a bath that evening). We did not bother to order our food from the hotel, if the rooms were as bad, we could only imagine what the kitchen would have been like. Once we threw all our bags into a corner, we walked outside to have food and make phone calls, only the government service providers, post-paid connections worked. Nobody amongst us had a government controlled "Bharath Sanchar Nigam Limited" or BSNL phone with us. We walked into an STD (Standard Truck Dialling) booth to make calls home. The first one was not working; there was something wrong with the system. So we walked to the only other booth in town, there was one phone that used the same system as the phone in the other booth used and it did not work here either. The second phone was a different system and we were able to make calls and let everyone know we were alive and well. On our way back to the hotel, we stopped at a restaurant for dinner. Nobody was hungry, so we all had a little rice and chicken curry. We washed it down with some tea and headed to bed. It was 8:00PM. We would start our last leg of the ride the next morning. We had ridden 275 kilometres from Leh to Drass and we were exhausted. Day 8 was over.

DAY 9

May 31, 2013

By 6AM we were up and ready to leave. Once we had all the bags tied down we rode out to just outside the gate and stopped for tea. While we sipped our hot, sweet tea the tea stall owner came up and started to speak to us. He was a native of Dehra Dun, and has never gone back after the beauty of Drass took hold of his imagination. He was there during the 1999 war and unlike most of the local population, he did not move to safer places. He instead chose to stay back and serve hot tea to the soldiers when they returned after the battle. He pointed out spots on the mountains behind his stall where the Indian Army and Pakistan army had outposts and that was at almost 20000 ft. and were nothing but small tiny dots to us. On the other side, he showed us huge craters on the mountain side that was made by the constant shelling. The craters were more than ten years old and had not yet covered up. He also mentioned that the hotel we stayed in last night was completely destroyed in the shelling and the buildings we occupied were reconstructed after the war. We stood for a while looking around us and I tried to picture the place as a war zone. We paid the man and started out. It was about a hundred and forty kilometres to Srinagar. We knew it would take more time than usual because of the mountain passes we would have to cross. When we left Leh, one of the men at the hotel advised to withdraw sufficient cash because ATMs are very few and far apart. We were still on National Highway 1 and would be on it, all the way to Srinagar. This stretch of road is generally closed for about six months of the year, usually from November to May because of the heavy snowfall, and when they do open are in pretty bad shape and the BRO has to start working immediately to clear all the snow out of the way and fixes any bridges that may have got damaged and repair the road as best as they can, and usually by mid-May or early June the road is thrown open to traffic. It was on this very stretch that there was the landslide that closed the road for two days. A major cause of delay on this highway is trucks, both army and oil tankers. They travel in huge convoys and end up blocking roads for hours on end. All this havoc is created by the very well known 'Zozli La' or 'Zojila', it is a mountain pass and tops off at about 11500 ft. It is the second highest pass on the road after the Fotu La that we had crossed the previous day. A very interesting fact we learnt from the man at the tea stall in Drass was that the Zozila was actually captured by Pakistani armed forces in 1948, but was soon re-captured. The Srinagar side of the pass gets lots of rain fall in the monsoon and is very dangerous and difficult to commute, the Drass side barely gets any rainfall at all and this is very evident from the quality of the road. The ride up to the pass was fast and pleasant. On the top we stopped to take pictures, the first time we had voluntarily stopped on top of any mountain. It was not too cold and the sun was up, busy polishing the ice off the mountain tops, making them glisten like huge diamonds in the sky. We finished taking pictures and looked at the road ahead, my heart skipped a beat. It was all wet and muddy and just big enough for a truck and car to squeeze past. I figured it was just that one small stretch, but as we rode, we could see that the whole road ahead was like that, we soon realized that it was because of the rain! We put two and two together and soon realized that on all passes, one side was good and the other side of the mountain would be bad. Now we knew why. As we started the descend, the progress became increasing difficult, there was way more traffic on this road than we had seen on any of the others so far and everybody wanted to cross over to the other side. Unlike the other passes we had crossed, this one had a considerable amount of heavy vehicle traffic. The petrol tankers took up more than half the road and because they were all going down empty, after having delivered their loads, they were all going faster than they should have. It soon became evident why the trucks would tear up the mountain while they were going north. Being fully loaded, the trucks coming up the pass have to maintain traction and the only way to do it is to maintain enough speed; they have to drive fast enough so that they do not lose traction and not too fast that the wheels lose contact with the uneven road. They would not slow down for anyone once they committed to a climb and the smaller vehicles in their path had to scramble out of the way. As we kept ridding down, the road started getting worse, because the temperature was higher and it was melting the snow quicker. After a while we came up on a truck that was almost blocking both lanes of traffic and there was a person under the hood trying to fix something. The people around the truck asked me to stop and wait. When I asked what happened, he told me that, as they were coming up, an inexperienced driver of a car stopped in front of them for no reason and to avoid a collision, the truck driver had to stop. He had lost all his momentum and ideally would have to back down far enough from where he would be able to drive up, gather enough momentum and cover the distance, but traffic was backing up behind him and he had no other option other than to try and pull up from a dead stop in the middle of a climb, and in doing so the inevitable happened. The axle of the truck broke under the strain and now everybody was stuck till the axle could be fixed or the truck moved out of the way. Throughout the pass, there are a few recovery trucks of both the army and the BRO, but none of these could reach the truck because of all the traffic that had backed up. On one side was the mountain itself and the other side a sheer drop. There was absolutely no gap between the truck and the mountain side, but there was a little space on the other side, wide enough for a motorcycle to pass. I weighed my options and decided to go for it. As soon as I started the motorcycle the men around the truck told me to stop and wait. One miscalculated move would send me and my motorcycle plummeting down the mountain, a certain death for both of us. But I insisted and so they decided to make a human chain and stand between me and the edge of the road. To be completely honest, I would not have done such a thing for a total stranger, someone who they would never ever see again. I even pointed out to them, that there was no way they could stop me and the motorcycle from going over the edge if something went wrong, the weight would be too much for a few people to hold back. However, they insisted saying that I was a guest of their state and nothing must happen to me. I was thoroughly impressed and slowly began to creep forward and in a few quick seconds was on the other side. I honked a thank you and a goodbye and continued on my way down. The truck would have been stuck for at least an hour because the traffic was backed up for about two kilometres. Thankfully everybody knew it was better to wait in line than to try and overtake and then make things worse. Again, I had pulled away from the other two and waited at the bottom of the pass. The scenery was breath taking and I just sat by the side of the road taking in the sights and sounds, the only sound of course was the wind and then there was the sound of sheep that were busy bleating on the mountain side as they were chewing the lush green grass. The sun was out and everything was warm and pleasant, it was an awesome day to just sit and while away time. In a few minutes the others caught up and we all sat and did nothing. Nobody spoke a word; we just looked across the valley at the snow topped mountain we had just crossed. That was the last mountain we would ride over for the rest of the trip. We were a little under a hundred kilometres from Srinagar. Now that the challenging part was over and the adrenaline subsided, our stomachs began to grumble and rumble for food. We set off in search for a place to eat, we stopped at a place called Sonamarg and had our breakfast; again, there was Maggie and tea. In front of the hotel were two young men, who were a part of the Taxi Owners Association and their primary job was to stop all cabs going towards Kargil and check if they had paid the appropriate fees. They were very curious about our motorcycles and walked around them, sat on them and then started asking questions about the motorcycles, the first; of course being what was the fuel efficiency. The two men had not ridden anything bigger than a 150cc motorcycle and were thoroughly impressed. We also had actually observed from the day that we started riding that many of the people along the road would wave out and smile at bikers; while on the other hand, they did not even take a second look at a cab full of tourists. Something about a motorcycle made most people wave out to us. We also came across people who would stop their cars and enquire from where we were riding and how long it was taking us, some even inviting us to stay at hotels or tents that they ran. We continued on towards Srinagar, stopping in between to buy a little petrol. This time however, we did not top up the tanks because we knew that our ride would end in a couple of hours and any excess petrol in the tanks would go to waste. In about two hours we were in Srinagar. It was not cold any more, rather it was hot but maybe that was because I was wearing thermal wear, two t-shirts and a nice thick jacket, which was necessary in Drass when we left that morning. Our goal was to find a company that would transport our bikes to Hyderabad. We called a telephone directory service and got the number of a few companies and called them all one by one. Srinagar is a big town and we knew we would have to search for the warehouse. From there we planned to take a bus or train to Delhi. As soon as we entered Srinagar, Akash spotted a large empty field and along its side was a row of buildings that looked like warehouses for logistics companies. We rode into the first company and asked them how much it would cost. It was a very reasonable ten thousand six hundred for the motorcycles going to Hyderabad and six thousand for the motorcycle going to Bangalore. It was cheaper than the quotes we got over the phone and three thousand rupees lesser than the amount we paid to get the motorcycles till Delhi. The name of the company is 'Nitco Logistics'; they are a reputed company with a footprint all over India. We do not know the reason for this huge difference in cost, but we were happy and decided to find a hotel, leave our luggage there and then come back, leave the motorcycles with the shipper. We left towards town to see what options we would have to leave Srinagar. We reached the tourist center and found the Srinagar Taxi stand. Akash and Srikant went to enquire about the rates and other information. It was May 31st, the last working day of the month, the day our salaries are credited to our accounts. We were eagerly waiting for the money, we were very short on cash and this fresh influx of money would make life much more easier for us. Almost every month the salary gets credited to our accounts by around six in the evening, that day however, the money was in our accounts by 4:30PM. Coincidence or luck I do not know, but we were mighty happy. We called and soon found out that there was a flight to Delhi at 5:30PM, I suggested we try and get it, but everyone else was sure we would miss it, considering we were yet to get our motorcycles to the shippers warehouse. I still was not very keen to sit in a cab or bus, so suggested staying over in Srinagar and flying out the next day, but when we checked the cost of the tickets, it was way too high and it would completely throw us off our budget. So we finally decided to take a cab to Jammu and from there a bus to Delhi. We spoke to a man at the taxi stand and he agreed to drive us to Jammu for about 5000 rupees (If my memory serves me correctly). We asked the cabbie to follow us as we doubled back to the warehouse as fast as we could, we wanted to get out of Srinagar as soon as possible, only then would we be able to get a bus out of Jammu that night. It is about three hundred kilometres to Jammu and takes about six hours and is National Highway 1A. We had enough and more time.

In the winter and monsoon these roads become very treacherous because of the numerous landslides and avalanches at a few places. We waited for what felt like an eternity while we got the paper work sorted out for all three motorcycles, we paid the amount and got into the cab and set off. It was a Chevrolet Tavera and we were comfortable in it. It was the first time we got to sit and relax while somebody else drove. The driver was an elderly man who kept telling us interesting facts. The one I found the most interesting was about 'saffron', they are a speciality to the area and grows only in a particular belt of Srinagar. The saffron grown in Srinagar is world famous and compared to the saffron grown in Iran, which incidentally falls in the same belt. A little later we all started feeling hungry, by the time we started, it was well over seven hours since we last had anything to eat, that is when we noticed that the driver would only stop at places he wanted to, we soon realized that the hotels would pay him a little money or not charge him for the food, if he got his passengers to the hotel. It was annoying considering that we were paying him and not the other way around. We let him know we were hungry, he said he knew a restaurant where the food is great and it would take us about half an hour to get there. We agreed, but that half an hour took more than an hour. When we finally did reach, the food was abysmal, but being as hungry as we were and not wanting to waste time going to another restaurant, we had rice and chicken curry before we all boarded the cab to continue on to Jammu. We next stopped at a check post where our driver went to pay the fee, the minute he stepped out, the car was swarmed by hawkers trying to sell their wares to gullible tourists. They were selling cherries, apples, strawberries and shawls. It all looked nice, but the way the men were putting their heads and hands into the car was a little over whelming and we pushed them out and locked the doors till the driver came back after which we continued on our way. A little later we came upon a tunnel, it was guarded by the army and photography was strictly prohibited. It was the 2.4 kilometre long "Jawahar Tunnel", it is over half a century old and the architects were German. The tunnel of course was renovated by the BRO sometime later and many modern features were added. The whole length of the tunnel is covered by CCTV cameras and stopping is prohibited. However, in the unlikely event that a vehicle breaks down while it is in the tunnel, there are telephones placed along the length of the tunnel for a stranded person to call for help. The original tunnel was a single tunnel designed for about 700 vehicles, now there are two parallel tunnels, one for traffic going north, and the second tunnel for traffic going south. It was around 7:30 in the evening and it was beginning to get dark. We had been riding since morning and sitting simply now was making me restless and bored, I soon fell asleep. When I woke up next, we were not moving, it was a traffic jam and a traffic jam in these mountains have stranded people for days. We stayed put in a place for about half an hour and then traffic slowly began to creep forward. A couple of minutes later we saw the cause for all the commotion. There were buffaloes on the road and not one or two, they were in the hundreds. We asked our driver what was happening and what he told us was the funniest thing I had heard since we started the trip. Every year when winter sets in, all the buffaloes in Srinagar are herded down to Jammu where the weather is obviously warmer. Now considering that there are no trains to Jammu from Srinagar, the only other way is by road. The roads however, are too dangerous and more than 85% of the road is in the mountains and many of the animals would get hurt or die in the constant rolling in the trucks. So then the only alternative left is to walk them and that is how it has been done for years. It is not very difficult to imagine. Picture this, a winding two lane mountain road, just big enough to let tucks pass and in between all of this large herds of buffalo ambling up the road and the worst part is they do not even care if an impatient motorist is honking behind them. They will walk at their own pace, stopping where and when they like. The herdsmen too, do not seem to bothered, I guess it is because there is nothing much they can do about it. These hundreds of buffaloes naturally cause traffic to back up and when they finally do move out of the way long enough for traffic to start moving, an overloaded tuck, unable to bear the strain of having to pull the heavy load from a dead start breaks down and makes a bad situation worse. All of this is tolerable, nothing can be done about the buffaloes or the broken down trucks. The most annoying elements in the traffic jam are impatient humans, when traffic is backed up, there will be at least one person who will think it is a smart thing to do and overtake all the other drivers who are patiently waiting for the road to clear, this selfish act by one person provokes others who also move out of the line, cross into the incoming lane and drive down only to make matters worse. Some people are forced to back up all the way to the top by other angry drivers. This particular line of backed up cars and trucks was well over five kilometres long, and we could see the ridiculously long line of traffic above us and snaking down below us. It actually looked pretty with all the lights lighting up the dark road, but after a while it all got too annoying and we were now very tired and we eventually fell asleep inside the car. The next time I woke up it was about half an hour to midnight and we were out of the traffic jam. Everybody else was fast asleep while our driver happily puffed away on his cigarette and listened to his old Hindi songs. When we had stopped for lunch the driver did not eat and now he said there was a place where the food was great. It was white rice with Rajma (a curry made with red kidney beans) and clarified butter or desi ghee. Thankfully unlike the previous restaurant, it was the best food we had eaten in a long time and thoroughly enjoyed ourselves. After we all ate and the driver had his fill, we started on our way. After sometime, the car slowed down, I had no clue for how long we had travelled or the distance we had covered since we had dinner. The reason we slowed down was a huge construction site, we were passing by that had dump trucks going in and out of the site. We learnt from the driver that it was the site of a major tunnel being built to cut travel down between Jammu and Srinagar by about fifty one kilometres. It was a twin tunnel about eight and a half kilometres long and, surprisingly was being built by the National Highways Authority of India (NHAI) and not the BRO. There was a large board put up beside the site with more details about the project, but we did not have the time to stop and read it. It was past midnight and technically day nine had come to an end. We started from Drass, reached Srinagar; got our motorcycles ready to transport back home and we were finally on our way to Jammu. The traffic jam caused by the buffaloes cost us six hours and we missed the bus from Jammu. There was nothing we could do but try and get some sleep. The only gain we had from the change in plan was that we did not have to stay in a hotel that night. Day 9 was over and yet, still not over.

DAY 10

JUNE 01, 2013

When I woke up next the cab was not moving and there was noise and activity all around us. It was 4:30 AM and we had finally arrived in Jammu. The plan was to find a bus headed for Delhi. The driver had stopped the cab in front of the bus stand and we went in to enquire. There were buses, but all the A/C buses departed only at night and we did not have that much time. The bus stand was crowded and dirty and we decided to leave. The driver suggested we check if trains are available. So then we headed to the railway station. A few minutes of our reaching there we realized that trains too would take us more time than we hoped. The next option was to hire another cab to drive us down to Delhi. It would be expensive and throw a wrench into our budget, but we had no option, so we bit the bullet and decided to hire yet another cab, because the cab that got us till Jammu did not have the necessary permits to cross the Jammu and Kashmir state line. It would cost us an additional thirteen thousand rupees and to our dismay we realized the vehicle hired was a sedan. It was going to be tight, cramped and uncomfortable. So we unloaded all of our stuff and reloaded it into the next vehicle and set off. It was around 6:30AM, by the time we finally started moving. Soon we were on the highway and on our way to Delhi. One by one we all fell asleep. We were about seventy kilometres out of town when the car began to sputter and cough. The driver pulled over and checked under the hood to see if he could trouble shoot the problem. The prognosis was bad, we had yet another delay. We slowly started to move again, after a while the driver informed us that we could not go much further without getting a mechanic to look at it. The highway was a major one and was dotted with many service stations and mechanics. However, it was so early, that none of them had opened as yet for business. We crawled our way to the border and our driver made a few calls and a friend of his, also a cabbie was returning to Delhi after dropping off his fare. He was waiting for us at the excise check post and once we reached, the drivers spoke for a while and reached a settlement on the price and for the third time in twenty four hours, we took all our bags out of one vehicle and bundled them into another. We started yet again, this time on a larger vehicle, the only benefit we gained from the previous cab breaking down. The driver was a short jolly man who kept talking non-stop. About an hour into the journey we stopped for fuel and then we started feeling hungry. The driver suggested he knew a great place and since he was the one who frequented the road, we decided to go with his judgement.

In about half an hour we reached the place he was talking about and soon understood why. There was a small area where he could have a bath and freshen up. So while he went about his business, we ordered food and as usual there was aloo parathas and a host of other parathas I have not heard about. The hotel, if I may call it so, was pretty new and only had a super structure with a few tables and benches scattered across the place. The only thing that was in plenty was flies. There were scores of them flying around our faces and on a normal day I would not go even near that place. Anyway, since the driver had already gone for his shower, we decided to order our food anyway. We knew it was going to take a while because we could see the cook starting to make the dough to roll out the parathas. By the time the food came, the driver was done with his shower and we were soon done and back on the road. As the day progressed it began to get hotter, the bigger factor being we were coming further down south. The driver offered to switch on the AC if we agreed to pay him a little more money. It seemed like a good idea and we began to bargain and soon settled on an additional four rupees for every kilometre we covered with the AC turned on. The roads were empty and in good condition and with the AC turned onto maximum we all started to fall asleep one after the other. All the days spent on the motorcycles without proper food and rest had taken its toll on us. A little later I woke hungry and ready to eat. The driver said there was a large mall we would cross in about half an hour and we should stop there for lunch. When we finally arrived, it was in the middle of nowhere, but was surprisingly crowded and bustling with activity. Most of the fast food chains had outlets there and after a quick trip to the washroom, we entered McDonalds and I soon settled into a hot McChicken and an ice cold Pepsi. We set off after the meal and soon fell asleep again. When I woke up in between everyone was asleep and I could see the drivers' eyes in the rear view mirror, he looked very drowsy, presumably because he had been driving all night with his previous passengers, I woke up Anoop and we both watched him for a while to see what was happening, thankfully he did not seem to be falling asleep and soon we drifted off back to sleep. In another few hours we were on the out skirts of Delhi and asked the driver to head to the airport, Akash wanted to see if there were any flights available so that he could fly home right away. We dropped him off at the airport and headed to town to find a hotel. We needed to have a long overdue shower and wait for our flight which was only the following day. We checked the prices in a couple of hotels before we decided to check-in to one that would cost us 1500 rupees per room, per night. It was within our now blown and recalculated budget. As we were unloading our stuff, we got a call from Akash, the tickets were too expensive and he booked a flight for early the next morning and was going to join us in the hotel. Once we had settled in, I decided I needed to get out of my boots. Other than the boots, I had no other footwear with me, so I set out to buy a more comfortable pair of footwear. The bell boy told me that a there were many stores down the road and I was on my way out, when Anoop said, he too wanted to buy a pair and together we were soon shoe hunting. The first store we came across was an Adidas showroom and we were in and out in less than ten minutes. On the way, I stopped, kicked my dirty boots off, left them by the road, put on my new comfortable sandals and headed back to the room. I had along hot shower and scrubbed myself clean and used about three sachets of shampoo and conditioner to clean the dirt out of my hair. We stepped out for dinner once all of us had our shower and then I went to bed, while the others went out for a couple of drinks. I stretched out on the bed, turned the AC on to its lowest setting and switched on the TV I watched for maybe an hour or so and before I knew it I was fast asleep. Day ten was finally over. We had been travelling for more than 24 hours. We started from Srinagar on May 31 at around 5:30PM and reached Delhi on June 1 at around 7:30PM.

DAY 11

JUNE 02, 2013

By the time we woke up, Akash had already left for the airport and was on his was to Trivandrum, via Mumbai. I was actually woken up by my phone ringing. A couple of colleagues who were in Delhi on official business, had missed their flight and had time to kill. Our flight was not until 5:00PM and so I joined the group for a movie. We watched Hangover 2 and then parted ways, their flight was also around five, but it was from the International airport or terminal 3, the same airport we landed at, on our way to Delhi from Hyderabad and our flight back to Hyderabad was from the domestic airport. I waited at the airport for Anoop and Srikant to arrive and once they arrived, we checked in and had a meal while we waited for the boarding call. Two and a half hours later I was back in Hyderabad and was at the end of our nine day road trip. It was good to be back home.

IN THE END

I have come to the end of my adventure I set out to tell you. We had a good run and count ourselves amongst the fortunate to have been able to ride through these beautiful roads and then walk out on our own feet and not be carried out on a stretcher. I would never have been able to write this book if it was not for the three wonderful guys who were a part of this exhilarating ride and I really believe a huge Thank you is definitely in order to Anoop, Akash and Srikant. Much of the credit for planning and making sure the ride went smoothly goes to Anoop; he painstakingly researched the routes and did most of the ground work. Srikant and Akash also were phenomenal fun to ride with and if I want to ride again, this would be the group of guys I would like to do this with. There were many things we could have done better, but all the research that was done did not actually detail out the kind of supplies or preparation we would require on such a trip. I have tried to compile a list of things that the others and I believe are essential and should be taken by anyone when going on a road trip, especially, if the roads are less travelled by others.

Apart from other essentials, a person who wants to make this trip by motorcycle should be carrying at a minimum the below listed items:

First and foremost on my list would be

1. Water Purification Pills: Dirty water can make a person very ill. (However, no water can kill sooner than dirty water, so the choice is between dirty water and no water, I would take my chances with dirty water)
2. A good tool kit: The one that comes with the motorcycle cannot fix all the problems. At the least it should include an air pump, screw driver set, pliers, flash light, spark plugs, electric/insulation tape and spare bulb
3. Riding gear: A good jacket that can keep the cold and heat out, a rain suit with reflective stripes for safe night riding. Being cold and wet will drain your energy and make you lose concentration, good sunglasses, with UV protection
4. Identification: A copy of all your vehicle documents and documents to prove your identity
5. Communication: A fully charged cell phone. In most mountains the phone will not work, but when you do reach a place with cell phone coverage; there should be enough power to make a call

6. A first kit that is more comprehensive than the kit that comes with the vehicle and should include a bottle of antiseptic cream, burn ointments, pain tablets, sterile bandages and an elastic bandage for sprain

7. A puncture kit, it should include patches, adhesive, extra tubes (some motorcycles have larger tubes for the rear wheel—make sure you have the right size).

8. Water tight boots: wet feet made me feel slippery (maybe it was just me)

9. Pack lightly and leave a little space to bring home some souvenirs

10. Above all, the love to ride. If you love what you do, you automatically start enjoying it

Make sure your motorcycle is in very good condition. It is very frustrating if you suffer a break down in the middle of nowhere because of a poorly maintained motorcycle. Break-downs cannot be completely prevented, but the possibility can be minimized by looking after the motorcycle. There is also a method advocated by the 'Motorcycle Safety Foundation', a United States based not-for-profit organisation founded in the early 70's by manufactures of high end motorcycles. It is called the "T-CLOCS" method and it is an effective way to inspect your motorcycle before starting the day's travel. It is this method that I followed during my walk around pre-trip inspections:

T: Tyres.

Make sure both tyres are properly inflated. Do not risk riding on tyres that might need replacement; if suspect a tyre will not last long enough for a ride, have it replaced.

C: Controls.

Are your cables (clutch and brakes) and controls intact and working?

L: Lights.

Make sure your headlights (high & low beam), turn signals, and brake lights work.

O: Oils & fluids.

Check everything from engine oil to brake fluid.

C: Chassis.

Ensure that the frame, suspension, chain, and fasteners are all secure and intact. Look for any lose nuts or bolts.

S: Stands.

Make sure the center stand and/or side stand is not cracked or bent, and that springs properly hold the assembly away from the pavement when stowed. If it were to hit the road while taking a bend at even relatively normal speeds, that will be sufficient to send both the bike and the rider tumbling head over heels.

There is far more comprehensive checklist available on the website of the foundation, but I generally follow the above method, it is quick and all essential or high risk parts of the motorcycle are covered.

I had said in the beginning that there is no other motorcycle we trusted to do the job and now at the end of it all, I am glad to say we had placed our trust well, because other than the two punctures, we did not have any mechanical troubles. If any of you plan to ride these roads, be prepared, because if you do not respect these roads, they will bite back and take you down. Many of people asked us if we would do it again. Definitely yes! I'm sure I will not be out of line, when I say that there will be things that we will do differently from how we did it this time. I am not at all surprised that there are people who make this trip every single year. There is a time to be born and a time to die, life follows death, just as death follows life, so it really does not matter where you end, as it all works out to the same thing, there were occasions when life hung by a thread, but for all these I feel amply rewarded to have been able to conquer some of India's toughest roads and ride wild and free in the beautiful country of India. We had ridden to the skies and come back safely. Ride safely, live well!